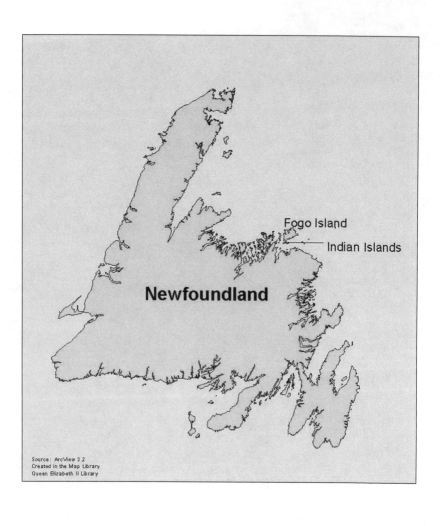

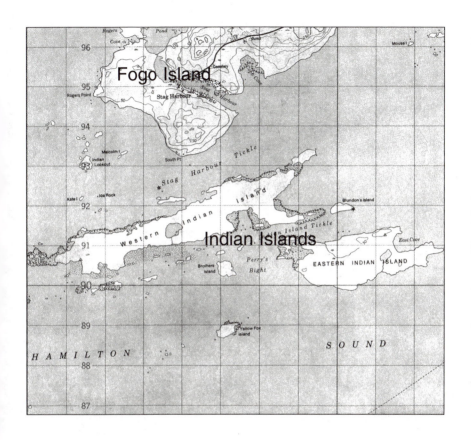

Always A Straight Shooter

by
Harold Collins

Always A Straight Shooter

Library and Archives of Canada Cataloguing in Publication

Collins, Harold, 1925-
    Always A Straight Shooter / by Harold Collins.

Includes index

ISBN 0-9684209-5-8

FC2175.1.C64A3 2004   971.8'04'092   C2004-903159-7

Front and Back Cover painting by St. John's Artist Audrey Cole

PRINTED IN CANADA

~ DRC Publishing ~

3 Parliament Street
St. John's, Newfoundland and Labrador A1A 2Y6

Telephone: (709) 726-0960
E-mail: staceypj@avint.net

Table of Contents

Foreword ix

Chapter 1 to 19 My Boyhood on Indian Islands 1

Chapters 20 to 39 My Work Life 73

Chapters 40 to 48 My Political Life 154

FOREWARD BY FRANK MOORES

For centuries, Newfoundland was a very tough environment in which to earn a living, raise a family and acquire any of the amenities that we take for granted today. Harsh weather in a harsh land was a way of life, as was economic hardship.

From this background, we like to believe that Newfoundlander thrived under austerity and amazingly, this was often true. We like to visualize the character of our people as one where hardship was overcome by humour and kindness to and from neighbours, sharing the few material things they had and looking after the elderly and the ill. From within this community Newfoundlander created their own entertainment and developed respect and trust- usually under the umbrella of deep religious faith. While this was not, always the case, for the vast majority it was.

No one I know represents the essence of the Newfoundland character more than does the author- Harold Collins.

Indian Islands, located in Notre Dame Bay off the northeast coast of Newfoundland, is windswept from all directions and gives the word isolation a whole new meaning. The only means of transportation was by open boat trough treacherous seas. But there was another side to Indian Islands. It was located in the middle of rich fishing grounds and the people had a fierce pride in their community. Through hard work and helping each other, they developed a resiliency that was unique in its time and doesn`t exist anywhere today.

This was where Harold Collins was born in 1925.

I am confident that Harold Collins will tell you there was much more happiness than there was misery and that hardship was overcome by the collective spirit and sacrifice of the community at large.

He left school at 14 to earn a living. He was fortunate to get a job with Department of Post & Telegraphs and his first posting was to Harbour Deep, a town nestled beneath the cliffs on the east coast of the northern peninsula. Harold had moved from a very isolated community to an even more isolated community.

Over the decades that followed, Harold worked in many communities around Newfoundland. I first met Harold Collins in Gander in the 1960`s. Even though he had been in Gander a short time, he was already one of the most popular persons in town. Always in good humour and with a sharp wit, he dove headlong into every charity around- whether it was hockey, baseball, the Boy Scouts or any other organization where he could help. It was obvious that the values and principles he learned in Indian Islands as a boy were still alive and well in the man. Yet with all that Harold Collins had done, he was about to make a contribution to Newfoundland way beyond what anyone could visualize.

When Newfoundland joined the Confederation in 1949, it was led by Joseph R. Smallwood, who remained the Premier until 1971. Smallwood ruled with an iron fist from the beginning, and with each year that passed, he became even more dictatorial. Anyone who spoke out against the Government was often fired if they were a government employee or if they worked for companies with government contracts. It was a period of intimidation and fear in Newfoundland.

A by-election was called in Gander in 1967. Harold Collins courageously stepped up as the P.C. candidate and to virtually everyone's surprise, he was elected. This was a major blow to Smallwood's dominance. The P.C.'s always had some support in St. John's but outport Newfoundland was rock solid in supporting Smallwood. Many look at the 1968 federal election, when the P.C.'s won 6 of 7 seats, as the event that turned the tide against Smallwood. But it was Harold Collins's victory in 1967 that initiated the demise of Smallwood's domination of Newfoundland politics.

When the P.C.'s formed the provincial government in 1972, Harold Collins was one of the first ministers appointed. He served in seven portfolios, including the major portfolios of Health, Fisheries and Municipal Affairs and Services, until his retirement from politics in 1979. Harold was dedicated and steadfast in each portfolio for which he was responsible. He was the voice of reason and common sense in Cabinet. he was the one person you could always depend on to be objective and voice concerns and aspirations of the common man. Harold never forgot his roots.

After leaving active politics, Harold was appointed Chairman of the Federal Fisheries Support Board where he served with distinction.

Harold is now retired and living in St. John's with Joan his wife of 54 years- the proud parents of seven boys and three girls and doting grandparents to 14 grandchildren.

Harold Collins epitomizes the Newfoundland character as we would want it to be. Rarely does an individual so capture the essence of a place, and a people, within his own personality. I know you will enjoy Harold's story.

~ Chapter One ~

I entered this world in the spring of 1925. My place of birth was Indian Islands, located on the northeast coast of Newfoundland and Labrador in Notre Dame Bay, and consisting of two islands named Western Indian Island and Eastern Indian Island. In the spring of the year the sun, which had gone south for the winter, was gradually returning to Indian Islands and its warmth was being felt. The ice, which for months seemed to be an extension of the islands, was beginning to lose its grip. It weakened, broke into pieces and melted or drifted away. The tickle between the two islands was transformed into water again and was navigable by boat.

However, while the harbour ice was gone, taking with it the tracks of men and horses from the winter activities, other obstacles were about to create more havoc. The dreaded Arctic ice which was now flowing south had jammed the tickle between the islands and travel between the islands became almost impossible. This posed a real dilemma for my grandmother, who was the practicing midwife for the community. My mother was pregnant and due to deliver at almost any moment. Another woman, Ethel Perry, who lived on the west island, was also due to deliver around the same time. I was told that my grandmother delivered me and immediately afterwards every available man was employed to transport her to the other island where Cyril Perry was delivered about an hour later. That was May 21, 1925.

My paternal grandparents, William and Elizabeth (Gosse) Collins, both of Spaniards Bay, represent the first generation of my family on Indian Islands. They moved to the islands in 1845, the year they were married. and settled on some of the best agricultural land on the East Island. The land consisted of three granted parcels, a total area of approximately five acres. My grandparents had four sons, William, Josiah, Richard and my father, Lorenzo, who was born in 1872.

My maternal grandparents were William Edgar from Harbour Grace and Mary Ann (Johnson) Sheppard of Seldom Come By. They had a family of twelve children, Kenneth, Martha, Mathilda, Moses, Mahalia, Herbert, Stephen, Winnifred, Allan, Edgar, Madilla and my mother, Bessie, born in 1888.

My father, Lorenzo, married Lydia Frampton and they had three children: Albert, born 1904; Mabel born 1906 and Muriel born in 1910. My mother, Bessie, married Allan Frampton and they were parents of four children: Harvey 1912, Lydia 1914, Meta 1917 and Kenneth 1919.

My parents both became widowed and they married each other in 1923. I was born in 1925, the only child of their union and the youngest brother of seven older siblings..

My father was an expert cod trap designer and builder. He built his own boats and made his own household furniture. Timber for the boats was procured from Fogo Island or across the Hamilton Sound in Carmanville or Frederickton. Logs for planks were harvested in the same places. The boat timbers were shaped with an axe and the plank was sawn with a pit saw. Much of the material used in making furniture was garnered from wooden crates used for packaging dried fruits, tea and other food stuffs.

My father was very active in community affairs. He was the chairman of the roads board and the school board, church warden, justice of the peace and postmaster. His advice and council was sought by many and was freely given. He provided tremendous community leadership.

My mother operated a small convenience store, selling sewing cotton, candy, chewing gum, life savers, sugar, biscuits and many other items needed on a day to day basis. She boarded the school teacher, assisted with washing and drying the summer catch of cod-fish, tended the vegetable gardens, and cut and dried grass for hay for the animals for the winter months.

Both she and my father were very kind and compassionate people. I can remember on many occasions in the spring of the year when some people's food supplies had been exhausted, my father and mother would gladly share flour, molasses, clothing and tobacco with their less fortunate neighbours. These qualities had a lasting effect on me and I have always strived to emulate them. My father died in 1957. My mother passed away in 1975.

~ Chapter Two ~

Where is Indian Islands?

The settlement of Indian Islands dates back to William Cull of Barr'd Island, Fogo Island, who established a home in Eastern Cove in 1810. Newfoundland governor Holloway had employed Cull to obtain information on the native Indians of Newfoundland. The name Indian Islands probably comes from the Beothuk Indians who yearly paddled down the Gander and Exploits rivers and out the bay to the islands for fishing. I am told there is evidence that the Indians lived in WigWam Cove near Eastern Cove.

My research indicates the islands were settled primarily by people from Conception Bay, in particular by people from Harbour Grace, Western Bay and Spaniards Bay. Many people from these communities took part in the Labrador schooner fishery. En route to Labrador, they often encountered heavy Arctic ice which blocked the passages through Stag Harbour Run and Hamilton Sound. While waiting for the ice to clear, they discovered fish in abundance at Indian Islands and some crews stayed there to fish all summer. After meeting with much success they decided to relocate there.

People often ask me "Where is Indian Islands?" and I tell them, "Well, the settlement was comprised of two islands referred to as the West and East Indian Islands. They are part of a group of many islands situated in the mouth of Gander Bay between Fogo Island and the mainland community of Carmanville."

The islands' profile is very low, the highest peak being no

more then 10 feet above sea level. On approaching the islands, the first thing to come into view were the houses and stages, leaving a stranger to think the buildings were afloat as was stated by a teacher named Lawrence in 1945.

The west island is locally referred to as Perry's Island because a number of families with the name Perry lived there. The east island, where my family lived, is a much smaller island but it contained many more people. The narrow strip of water between the islands was referred to as the Tickle and served as the harbour for the fishing boats and schooners, and the anchorage for the freight and mail service boats.

All of the Labrador fishing schooners and other coastal boats moving up and down the east coast passed through Stag Harbour Run. The large oil tankers destined to Lewisporte and the ore and paper carriers out of Botwood passed through Hamilton Sound where the water was much deeper.

The west end of our island was called Chalk's Cove and the shore line was all sandy beach. The east end of the island was made up of the small community of Eastern Cove and WigWam Cove and the beaches there were pebbly. In summer, vegetable gardens, grassy meadows, fish drying flakes and peat bogs where the bakeapples grew dominated the landscape. The water was generally calm and teeming with caplin, cod, salmon and lobster. Fishing activity was intense and life was pleasant.

When summer ended and the fall of the year approached, drastic changes occurred. The calm and pleasant southwest breezes of summer were replaced by northerly and northeast gales.

The tickle could no longer provide protection for the boats and they had to be moved to Clay Island Tickle on the west end of the island, or taken out of the water as the fall storms become more severe. It was not uncommon for fishing wharves and stages to be severely damaged and sometimes completely washed away.

Navigation came to an abrupt end around the end of the year and brought with it the beginning of winter. My recollection is that the land was completely snow covered. Sometimes the drifted snow was level with the roof of the houses and neighbours were required to shovel each other out because people inside the houses could not get out. The surrounding shoreline became an endless ballicatter (ice formed by spray on the shore). The bay ice seemed to be welded to the rocks and the Northern Lights, which looked like "the furniture of the sky," provided the only sense of shelter. We were then virtually in a very savage environment.

~ Chapter Three ~

Growing up

When I was growing up, everyone fished in summer mainly using cod traps. Some people supplemented their earnings by going to the lumber woods in the fall. They generally went to Millertown, Badger, Bishop's Falls and across the country, as they would say, to Deer Lake. Still others continued the fall hook and line fishery at Little Fogo Islands. These islands stand out in the Atlantic off the east of Fogo Island. Many people maintained substantial premises on these islands. Our establishment at Eastern Tickle consisted of a camp, stage and wharf.

I remember the people of my childhood as hard working and God fearing. They had a great respect for the sea and knew precisely to what extent they could master it. They had a fierce independence and a great ability for improvisation. Their native ingenuity enabled them to cope with just about any circumstance, and coupled with this was a great spirit of sharing with and helping each other. This created very close family and community relationships.

I left Indian Islands in 1939. I returned a few times for short summer vacations and again shortly after resettlement of the 1950's. At that time, the only remains of a once proud and thriving community were a number of run down houses, stores and stages. The unkempt cemeteries and a fading stone monument to the victims of the First World War stirred memories that will not be easily erased from my mind.

Not unlike children in other small coastal areas, my brothers, friends and I played a form of baseball and kick football in the summer. In winter, we played hockey on the pond on the island. We jigged tom cod on the stage head and had great bonfires on November 5. We picked bakeapples in the summer and sold those excess to our family's needs to the crew of the mailboat, Glencoe, for 25 cents a gallon. As well as bakeapples, we picked partridge berries, blue berries and marsh berries, all of which were a tremendous source of vitamin C, although we didn't know that at the time.

By the time children reached the age of eight, life took on a very different meaning. While there was still time for play, there was work to be done. Everyone in the family was required to shoulder certain responsibilities in the name of survival. My mother always referred to it as keeping body and soul together, in other words eking out a living.

We didn't have the luxury of running water in our house. Water for household purposes was stored in a wooden barrel on the back platform. In the winter, the barrel was relocated to the inside and, even then, on cold nights the water in it would freeze over. One of my responsibilities was to keep the water barrel filled. There was a public well not too far from where we lived and about ten families drew their water from it. The water was of a very good quality and drawn from the well by means of a three gallon bucket attached to a rope. The water was transferred to two other buckets and with the help of a round hoop to even the weight and keep the buckets upright, it was carried home and poured in the family barrel. It would take about five trips to fill the barrel. In winter time the water was hauled home on a sleigh. Rainwater was collected and used for laundry purposes.

Our house was equipped with two stoves, a large stove in the kitchen and a smaller wood burning stove in the parlour. We only saw the inside of the parlour when the clergyman or some other VIP. was visiting. The stove in the kitchen was a "Waterloo" that burned wood and was the sole source of heat for the house. It was also used for cooking and baking and was equipped with an oven, a warming closet and a water tank. Maintaining a good supply of wood in the box behind the stove was one of my responsibilities.

In the back garden, far removed from the house, was our barn and hayloft. We had a horse, a mare named "Queen," four sheep, two goats, eight or ten hens, a rooster, a pair of ducks, and two pigs. All the animals were kept in the barn in the winter months and let loose in the spring, the one exception being the hens, which were secured in a suitable enclosure for the protection of the eggs. In winter, I assisted my father in feeding and watering the animals and the daily cleaning of the stalls in the barn. The horse was used for hauling wood from Fogo Island during the winter freeze-up and hauling kelp and animal manure to the gardens in the spring. The goats were used for milk and the sheep for wool, which my mother used for knitting socks, mitts and sweaters and caps. The sheep and the goats, along with the horse, roamed the island at leisure during the spring summer and fall. Houses and gardens were fenced not to keep animals in, but to keep them out.

The centre of the island contained some very dangerous bog lands. When cows were first introduced to the island they were attracted to the bogs by the grasses which grew there and suddenly became bogged down and lost. As an alternative source of milk, goats were introduced and they thrived on the islands as long as people lived there. Rounding up the goats for milking twice a day was another of my chores. While my mother milked the goats, I kept them occupied with treats from the kitchen. My mother always saved the vegetable peelings exclusively for that purpose.

To feed the hens, corn was brought in from St. John`s and supplemented with scraps of leftover foods from the kitchen. Sometimes the kitchen scraps contained small portions of fatback pork. While feeding the hens one day I noticed that when the hens swallowed a piece of pork it was ejected out the other end almost immediately. In what my mother called a cruel exhibition of badness, I tied a piece of pork to one end of a long piece of string and threw it in among the hens. Quickly a hen swallowed it and just as quickly it ejected it. In no time, another hen did the same thing, and in no time flat I had all the hens on a string. Mother knew what was happening and she didn't think what I had done was funny. She insisted that I release the hens. The birds showed no ill effects from the ordeal.

I never mentioned this to anyone until one night a few years ago. I was watching television and a reporter was interviewing

Hollywood movie star Gregory Peck who was in Vancouver shooting a film. I became interested in the interview when the reporter asked Peck about his upbringing on a farm. Peck reminisced about it and one of the stories he told was of getting the hens on a string. Since it was the same thing as I did, and he told it on national television, I suppose there is no harm in relating my story here.

I remember one sunny summer day when my mother had been up for some time doing various household chores and preparing breakfast for my father and my brother, Harvey, who were expected to arrive in an hour or so. They had left home around 3 a.m. to haul one of the cod-traps set at the southern point of Fogo Island, an area referred to as the Cape.

It was approximately 7 a.m. and I was still in bed when I heard my mother calling to me. She said, " It's such a nice calm morning and I want you to get up and go out in the boat and get some lumpfish and flatfish for the pigs."

Like most families. we kept two pigs for slaughter in the fall. The pigs were fed a substantially fish diet until just before slaughter when they were given a cleaning or finishing concoction which supposedly purged the animal of what could be a fishy taste.

I stumbled out of bed, adjusted my eyes to the brightness of the sun, opened the window drapes, pulled on some clothes, and went down to the kitchen. In order to answer nature's call, I put on my boots and went outdoors to the outhouse, which was located on the landwash side of the road over the water. Upon returning to the kitchen, I headed to the corner wash basin and the invigorating shock of cold water which my mother had taken from the water barrel. After I cleaned my teeth I sat at the kitchen table and enjoyed a good Newfoundland breakfast of fried bologna, eggs, toast and tea .

As I was leaving, my mother implored me to be very careful, she always seemed concerned that I might fall overboard. I headed for the stage and the small punt which was tied to the wharf. I had a long pole with me, one end of the pole was equipped with a spear and a hook. The spear was used to stab the flatfish and the hook to retrieve the lumpfish. I had a successful morning and by the time I returned and fed the fish to the pigs, my father and Harvey had arrived from the Cape with nearly a boat load of codfish. The remainder of the morning was spent in helping process the codfish.

~ *Chapter Four* ~

My Mother's Work Day

When I look back on the many notes I made over the years it never ceases to amaze me the amount of work my mother did back on Indian Islands. A normal spring and summer day found her out of bed around 7 a.m. After preparing breakfast for a group of hungry fishermen she would scrub the wooden kitchen floor with a hand brush, working on her knees. She mixed and baked bread every day. In place of yeast she used a barm. The barm was made in a bowl from a fermenting plant which she kept warm on a shelf behind the kitchen stove. When the barm was ready, it was mixed with the flour in a large mixing pan and left to rise. She would make sure she had a good fire in the wood stove and at the right time put the dough into baking pans then into the oven to bake. In addition to seven or eight three bun loaves, she would always make two or three single bun loaves. What a treat to be served these hot from the oven buns spread with Solo butter.

In the spring, my mother set seeds, then weeded and cared for the garden. We had two goats which had to be milked in the morning and again in the evening, and the milk scalded on the stove to cleanse it for use.

We had no running water and no washing machine. I would often help my mother take the dirty clothes out to the brook which ran by the garden. Kneeling on a flat rock and using homemade Lye soap she would scrub the clothes and then we would bring everything back inside the fence and hang it on the clothes line to dry. When the clothes were dry they were brought inside, ironed, and put away. Several other women used the same area for washing and it seemed to be a social gathering place.

By mid-summer, after there was a slackening in the fishery, our four or five sheep were rounded up and brought to the garden for shearing. I used to help keep the sheep under control while my mother using ordinary household scissors to cut off their wool. The wool was washed several times, dried and stored. Early in the fall the wool was carded — wool cards were devices that consisted of bent wire teeth set tightly in leather and backed with a wooden handle. With a card in each hand, and working in opposite directions, the wool was cleansed, disentangled, and made ready for spinning into wool. The spinning process converted the wool into thread called yarn. This process involved the use of a hand driven or foot driven wheel which was connected to a spindle by a belt. The spindle twisted the wool into string called wool yarn. My mother used 12 inch steel needles to knit mitts, socks, sweaters and sometimes underwear.

I never did try knitting, but I did help to hook mats. To hook a mat, my father constructed an adjustable wooden frame. Burlap, commonly referred to as "brin," was stretched and tied to the frame and provided the base for the mat. The next step was to outline a pattern on the brin. Condemned clothes were cut into suitable sized strips and pulled through the brin using a mat hook. Mats were used mostly as floor coverings. A large mat with " Welcome" written in the centre adorned the entrance to our back kitchen. Nailed on the step beside it was an old scrubbing brush used to remove dirt from the soles of footwear. The final scuffing took place on the welcome mat.

Knitting and hooking mats took place at night, with light provided by a kerosene lamp that was either placed on a table or mounted on a wall. Every room in the house had a kerosene lamp, consisting of a glass vessel filled with kerosene, and a burner with a wick mounted on the top of the glass vessel. The wick could be adjusted by means of a screw attachment. The amount of flame could be increased or decreased by adjusting the wick. The flame produced by the wick shone through a glass globe held in place by four brackets which were part of the burner. The sudden opening and closing of a door caused air disturbances which led the wick to burn more brightly, resulting in smoking. This caused the globe or, as we called it, the chimney to become clouded with smoke. Cleaning lamp chimneys was a daily routine and, depending how smoky the chimney was, sometimes soap and water was required. For the final cleaning and shining of the chimney we used an old newspaper. The wicks became hardened after a full night's use and this reduced the flow of oil. Most people used scissors to trim the wick. My mother always used a tool called a "snuffer" which was shaped like scissors and had very sharp cutting blades. On the reverse side of the blades were soft wire brushes. After the wick was cut, the brushes would loosen the fibres of the wick, improving the flow of oil. My mother's snuffer has found its place in our home and is now in my wife's kitchen.

~ Chapter Five ~

Memories of a Small Boy

It was early in June and I was nine years old, my birthday being May 21. Even though I was going to school I was expected, and indeed required , to do what I could to contribute and maintain our way of life. Similar demands were made of all children. To eke out a living everyone was expected to pull his or her weight.

Spring came early that year and, in the absence of northern ice, my father, brother Harvey, and the crew had set out a cod-trap in Otter Cove, just inside the South Bill of Cape Fogo, which was about nine miles from where we lived. The I'm Alone, our trap skiff, was equipped with an eight horse power Acadia engine which would take about an hour and half each way to the Cape.

The water could become very rough and treacherous depending upon the direction and force of the winds, and while there were no official forecasts like we have today many of the older people were reasonably accurate in their weather predictions.

Back then, the one and only forecast available was a long range farmer's forecast which was printed in the Family Herald, and just about everyone subscribed to that paper which was printed in Winnipeg, Manitoba.

I remember very well how my father predicted the weather. Just before he was ready to go to bed he would lay down his twine needle and go outdoors. After throwing away the wad of Beaver chewing tobacco he'd had in his mouth all evening he would invariably go across the road and down to the beach where he would examine the extent of the water-tow.

After careful examination of the sky and the type and direction of movement of the clouds, he would proceed to the wall in the house where the old brass barometer was hanging. With his forefinger, which resembled a gaff hook, he would gently tap and see which direction it was moving since the previous night. He could then pronounce whether tomorrow was going to be a civil day, meaning little wind, or if it was going to be stormy, and what direction the wind would be blowing. He would indicate whether it was going to be dry or wet and he was seldom wrong.

On this particular day, my father and the crew had left about 3 a.m. to motor to the Cape and haul the cod trap. It was still dark and the navigation light on Blundon's Island was flashing when I heard my mother calling me, "It`s time to get up, it`s going to be a nice day and I want you to help me in seeding the small vegetable garden."

The big garden which contained potatoes and turnips had already been planted by the men. It was now time to plant carrot, parsnip, lettuce and other varieties of seed, which she had ordered t from the Gaze Seed Company in St. John`s. It took a bit of persuasion on her part to get me to vacate the comfortable feather bed. As I dressed and stumbled downstairs I was met with the pleasant aroma of breakfast cooking and as soon as I had washed we sat and ate. We then proceeded to the small garden near the house. Using our horse, Queen, and the old two- wheeled cart my father had already hauled decomposed kelp and animal barn manure to the site. We got busy arranging the soil in beds, after the organic material had been mixed in, my mother planted her seeds. Before we finished we heard the sound of the I`m Alone approaching and my mother rushed to prepare breakfast for the returning hungry men. For me, it was off to school and a hard day's work in the classroom.

The following morning when my mother woke me I could hear the fog horn on the Island and it was a little damp outside, a great morning for gardening. Mother and I finished the seeding and we had a beautiful crop in the fall.

Before I was old enough to go fishing with a crew in the boat, I was expected to help in the processing of the fish. When the boat arrived from the traps, and after breakfast was eaten, the fish was removed from the boat by pronging it on to the wharf. The wharf deck was about 8 to 10 feet high, perhaps even higher at low tide, and the work was time consuming and arduous.

As the men pronged the fish upon the wharf, I helped move it inside the stage or kept it covered with canvas in order to keep the hot sun from spoiling it.

Once the fish was removed from the boat, the splitting began. In front of the splitting table a large box on legs was filled with fish and my job was to keep the box filled with fish to be processed.

Four men stood around the splitting table. The first man, called the " cut throater" would use his knife to cut the fish's throat and open the belly. The fish was then pushed to "the header" who removed the gullet and liver. The gullet or stomach was discarded, but the liver was dropped in a hole in the table to a barrel underneath. The fish was then passed to one of the splitters who removed the sound bone and dropped the fish in a wheel barrow of water. The fish was quickly washed and passed onto the salter who laid it in a pile as it was salted.

In the process of removing the gullet from the fish the header would very often inadvertently discard pieces of the liver. After the processing was over, I would recover these livers and sell them to Nick Perry, a local business man, who paid me about 20 cents per gallon.

My pay from the processing work was generally in the form of fish. In order to identify my fish. the tails were cut, that is, a small piece of the tail measuring about a square inch was cut away. As the fish were washed and dried in the fall of the year, mine could be identified by the tail markings. Such fish were commonly referred to as cut-tails.

In the early 1930s, my father was stricken with a crippling disease known as beri-beri, which is usually caused by certain vitamin deficiencies. As a result of his illness, he was forced to abandon the Labrador schooner fishery and devote his energy to the local cod trap fishery. The disease was so disabling and affected his knees so badly that he was finally forced to give up boat trips altogether.

My father was always a good worker at splitting codfish and could stand for as long as work had to be done, but with his condition he could do little. I helped out with chores such as planting the gardens and soon found myself taking his place in many endeavors.

My induction into the fishery occurred in 1936 when I was 11 years old. The Department of Education C.H.E. public exams were always written in the United Church School on Perry`s Island. I wrote the primary exam (Grade IX) that year and as soon as the last paper was written, I joined my brother, Harvey, who was now the skipper, and his sharemen and we proceeded to the fishing grounds. I remember the crew welcomed me aboard and Harvey said, "You`re a man now." Our three sharemen were Stanley Kinden, Jimmy Collins and Uncle Allan Sheppard, and Stanley said, "If you`re not a man now you will be one by the time the summer is over."

We had two cod traps, a small one and a large one. The small trap was already loaded in the skiff and we proceeded to a berth known as the Outside Sunker East of Grandfathers Island. The small trap was set there because the water depth was shallow, relatively speaking, about eight fathoms. The large trap was built for twelve fathoms of water and was later set in the Fish Gulch berth, which was located on the East side of the North Bill of Cape Fogo, near Bowling Pond Head.

Stanley Kinden was a grizzled, wrinkled man in his fifties but he looked and acted much older. Stanley was very gentle and kind. Jimmy Collins (no relation to me) was a mountain of a man with Coke bottle glasses worn on the bridge of his nose. He had a short fuse and when he was working hard his tongue extended out between his teeth and lips. On many occasions I thought he would bite off his tongue. The other side of him was very gentle but it would be a mistake to irritate him too much. Uncle Allan Sheppard , my mother's brother, was a real showman, he was very agile and strong, of average height and weight. At the drop of a hat, he could drop down and do a hundred push-ups and challenge anyone to do more. He used to kid Jimmy quite often and while Jimmy took it all in stride, at times I was more than a little bit scared. They all treated me well and made sure I didn't do things that might get me injured. Those men worked hard all their lives in the fishing boat and in the lumber woods.

The procedure in setting a cod trap was to put the moorings in place first, to be followed by the trap itself. The first mooring to be put in place was the shorefast. The rope was tied to the shore, or tied to a grapnel which was put close to shore. Rope was fed out until the skiff was located where the box of the trap would be set. The spanline was then connected and the rope for the back mooring attached and generally tied to an anchor and dropped in place. With the spanline now across the boat, the two back corners and the two front vee mooring lines and grapnels were put in place. The skiff was now anchored. A row boat or punt was used to position the other anchors. One anchor and the required amount of rope was loaded from the skiff to the punt. Uncle Allan, Jimmy and I manned the punt and on Harvey's direction we rowed the moorings out. Jimmy occupied the front seat and I occupied the second taut. As we rowed, Uncle Allan kept feeding the rope over the side making sure it did not become entangled. As more rope was fed overboard rowing became more difficult because the rope had to remain taut.

Uncle Allan was a one time Bowater Camp boxing champion and Jimmy was no weakling either. As we tried to stretch the mooring rope, Uncle Allan used to kid Jimmy by saying, " Jimmy, if you can't row harder than that, I'll have to put Harold in front and you will have to come back here." Jimmy was having none of that and, as he responded to Uncle Allan`s challenge, I could feel the punt shake from his strength of Jimmy`s arms. By the closing of the day all moorings were in place and the cod trap was set. That first day, I thought my legs would separate from the rest of my body and my hands were very sore from holding the oars and rowing, but after we arrived back home and ate a good meal cooked by my mother I was ready to go again. The next day we hauled both traps but took only a few fish and after some fine tuning on the moorings we left for home.

The caplin were now rolling in on all the beaches around the island and we devoted a full day to procure an adequate amount for salting and drying. Using the horse and cart, we hauled enough to the garden to provide the nitrogen the soil needed. The small fish were spread over the raised beds and covered with soil. This procedure was known as trenching and it was now a matter of time before the vegetables would grow.

A few days after the caplin came, the cod fish arrived and between the two traps we were getting all the fish we could process. One morning the trap at the Gulch contained more fish than we could take in our boat. The I`m Alone could take up to 25 barrels of fish, depending on the weather conditions. It was a calm morning and after loading the boat to the gunwales we had about 15 barrels left in the trap. Every skiff was equipped with a cod bag. It was made of four inch mesh and equipped with a draw string. The excess fish was directed to the bag and tied to the trap. We headed home and after breakfast, when the fish had been removed from the skiff, Harvey and I left to retrieve the bagged fish.

The wind was now from the southwest and blowing fairly strongly as we left the wharf. Harvey called to me, "Get the damned engine going or we are going to drift on the rocks."

In my rush, the engine caught in reverse and I knew I had hurt my arm. After reversing the engine to forward, we escaped the rocks and when I had the engine to what was the normal cruising speed I attempted to leave the engine house. In order to leave the engine room I had to take my weight on both arms on the stanchions which support the engine house. I couldn't place any weight on my right arm and was forced to sit in the house. Harvey eventually noticed something was wrong and implored me to leave the engine house. With his assistance I finally reached the deck and explained to him that my arm was really hurting. In no time it started to pain and become swollen. We knew the arm was badly hurt but thought it was not broken so we decided to continue to the trap. Harvey had to dip all the fish from the bag because my arm was really hurting. When all the fish has been removed from the cod bag, Harvey started the engine and we proceeded on our way home. It was late evening before all the fish was processed and my father brought his attention to my arm. He concluded that I should see a doctor and so at 11 p.m. Harvey and I left for Fogo to see Dr. MacKenzie at the medical clinic. The clinic was attached to his home and when we arrived the doctor had retired for the night. In no time he was up and we were admitted to the clinic. The doctors diagnosis was that the arm was broken just above the wrist. Because of the delay he had to reset the bone and put a cast on it. It was a very painful experience. My father paid him for his services and we left for home.

The next day was Sunday and we were supposed to go to church. Reverend Noel was visiting the island and he was staying for the weekend. By church time my arm was hurting more than ever and the swelling at both ends of the cast appeared a little frightening. George Collins, who was a great first aid man, was summoned and he declared the cast would have to be removed, taking great care to ensure the break was not disturbed. George proceeded to fit the arm with four splints, like pieces of kindling and carefully wrapped it together. Within a couple of days the excessive swelling had disappeared but I had to wear the splint all summer. I couldn't do much work, but I kept the men's tobacco pipes filled, made sure there was plenty of water on hand and helped the salter.

On Indian Islands, fresh fruits were expensive, available only in the summer, and not everyone could afford to buy them. Dried and canned fruits were more the norm, supplemented by wild fruits. The more common and most plentiful varieties were bakeapples, marsh berries, partridge berries, blue berries, raspberries and blackberries.

Squash berries and black and red currants were cultivated in private gardens. Black berries were very acid and required huge amounts of sugar to make jam edible so they were seldom used if other varieties were available.

The quantity and quality varied from year to year, but as a rule there seemed to be a more than ample supply of all berries most years. We ate freshly picked berries, and used them to make jams and jellies which were bottled and lasted year round. There was one exception to the rule and that was blueberries. Blueberry jam was never a favourite, so many of those berries were used to produce blueberry wine. There was some powerful stuff brewed, as mummers at Christmas could attest! In the early growing stage the blueberry was white. As it ripened, it turned red and then eventually blue when fully ripe. It was late in the fall and a danger of frost before all the berries were ripe. Rather than take the chance of losing the berries through frost, harvesting began before all the berries had ripened. People still pick these berries on fine days in September and October. They can be seen on the hill sides with their white salt beef pails and other containers picking berries. For convenience, two containers are almost always used, one small and one large. The small container is more convenient to hold while removing the berries from the bushes. When it is filled it is emptied into the large container.

I should relate to you the story about the American tourist traveling across Newfoundland by car in the fall . He noticed several people up on the side of a hill with their white containers. They were bent over obviously picking up something which they were putting in these containers. His curiosity got the better of him. He parked his car on the shoulder of the road and waited for the people to come down. When they did he observed the containers were filled with berries. He enquired as to the kind of berries they were, "Oh, them are blueberries, sir" volunteered one elderly lady, still holding her aching back. The American said "How come many of them are red?" "Sir," she said, "'because they`re green." That was rather confusing to the poor guy. He thought he was speaking to someone who didn't have all their marbles.

While exposure to frost ruined blueberries, it enhanced the quality of partridge berries and marsh berries. Partridge berries grow in bunches on vines on barrens and old cut overs are ideal growing areas. The berries resistance to frost damage meant they were left to ripen completely before they were harvested.

Marsh berries grew in the swampy areas, a single berry at the end of a hairlike stem protruding from the small plant. They were picked individually, berry by berry. It would take a long time to pick a gallon, but it was worth the effort. If they weren't preserved as jam they could be stored in water. The water seemed to enhance the ripening process and flavour.

In the spring, after the berries had ripened under snow and ice, we could pick them when they were quite red and full of juice. We considered marsh berries the queen of the berries.

If the marshberry was queen, the bakeapple was certainly the king. These prized berries were found on bogs, the dry peat bog variety, as opposed to swampy areas. People used to come across the Bay and from Fogo Island to pick these berries. Today I understand people from as far away as Lewisporte visit the Indian Islands for bakeapples. These berries were and are preserved as jam and are quite a delicacy when served as a dessert.

There were many disadvantages to living on a small island and perhaps the greatest was isolation. For instance, the nearest doctor was stationed at Fogo, a distance of some fifteen miles by sea. The nearest hospital was at Twillingate, some thirty miles away. Ice and treacherous seas presented a very real challenge to travel by boat, more especially in the spring and fall. Winter conditions brought the added risk of travel over ice.

Communications with the outside world was limited to a

weekly mail service, provided by the S.S. Glencoe, which was operated by the Newfoundland Railway and served ports between St. John's and Lewisporte. That service was reasonably reliable between June and December but after that navigation by sea became almost impossible and her Majesty's mail was dispatched by what was called the overland route. The main distribution point for our region was Lewisporte. The Boyd's Cove mailman brought the mail from Lewisporte to Boyd's Cove. The Fogo Island crew brought it to Fogo Island and our man operated between Fogo and Stag Harbour. The delivery of mail and provision of communication service was the responsibility of the Department of Posts and Telegraphs, which was modeled after the British system.

Wireless communications was introduced to the islands in 1934, when the post office was equipped with the necessary electronic equipment to permit the sending and receiving of messages by means of the Morse code. A lady named Florence Rowe of Seldom Come By was sent to the island to operate the system and she trained my sister, Lydia, who succeeded my father as postmaster. As Lydia gained confidence and became more proficient she trained my sister, Meta, and my brother, Kenneth. I took advantage of the informal training sessions and pretty soon the conversations in our house were conducted in Morse Code. It could be said that we enjoyed Morse Code for breakfast, dinner and supper.

In 1935, my father purchased a Zenith radio, the first on the island. It was operated on dry cell batteries. Many islanders would gather at our house at seven in the evening to hear the world news from radio station W.O.R. in New York. The reception was usually better at night due to certain atmospheric conditions. The local news was broadcasted by radio station V.O.N.F. from St. John's and it also attracted large audiences.

Before and after supper I would tune in Wheeling, West Virginia, and listen to country and western blue brass music and other songs. Another popular station was New Carlisle, Quebec. That was a luxury which did not rate highly with my parents because they were concerned the batteries would be drained by the time the news came on. These concerns were eliminated when we installed a wind charger and wet cell batteries.

~ Chapter Six ~

Christmas on Indian Islands

We began preparations for Christmas in early December. Christmas celebrations were centered around the home, the church and the community. All 12 days of Christmas were celebrated. While there were no large trees on the island, there was an ample supply of a ground cover called "evergreen." The foliage of this plant remained green and functional past the growing season and made it ideal for decorating. It was used as the chief decoration around the inside of the church and was as commonplace at Christmas as the palm leaf at Easter.

The school, which was the center of celebrations on Christmas eve, had a tree obtained from off the island. A small tree was also procured for the house. The old decorations from previous years were hung around and everything was in gladness for the big event. Adequate supplies of wood were sawn and split, kindling was made to ensure there would be no interruption to the celebration. The women baked buns and cakes and cookies and bread. Jams and other preserves were readied. Lots of syrup — a traditional non-alcoholic Christmas drink, red and sweet and diluted with water— was laid in. If we could afford a turkey it was ordered from St. John`s, if not, salt water ducks would provide the main course for Christmas dinner. Those who relished something stronger than syrup made molasses beer and moonshine. Those who could afford it, brought in two or three bottles of Dooleys or Bookers rum from the Board of Liquor Control. If we were lucky and there wasn't too much ice in Hamilton Sound , the Newfoundland coastal boat Glencoe would arrive. This last trip was generally around December 20, shortly before all the boats were hauled up and Christmas Eve arrived.

With the exception of some afternoon cheating, the first real Christmas celebration took place at the school house just after supper when children arrived and Santa distributed their gifts from underneath a beautiful decorated Christmas tree.

Carols were sung and a concert followed. When the children were tired they were taken home and the place was prepared for a square dance. Dancing went on until the wee morning hours.

On Christmas morning, there was communion at 11:00 a.m. and evening services at 8:00 p.m. and church was well attended . Other than feasting at home, little else took place on Christmas Day.

The next day, St. Stephen`s Day, now called Boxing Day, saw the real beginning of celebrations. People would visit each other in their houses, and at night mummering began in earnest. Young and old would dress up and go mummering. A house visit would generally involve a serving of cake and syrup, hard liquor or beer, if it was available. If the mummers were identified they would remove their veils, if not, they departed unknown for the next house.

Every conceivable sport was indulged in over Christmas. The older men often joined in with the young boys in rounders, football and other games. Much house visiting occurred and this was continued until New Year`s Day.

New Year`s Day was a time for children to visit their godparents. Mine were Aunt Floss Frampton and Aunt Helen Sheppard. Two darling women, long since passed to their reward.

I could always look forward to a pair of double knit, black and white wool mitts from both of them. Celebrations continued until Old Christmas Day, January 6. By then, all the goodies had been eaten. The beer and moonshine was all gone. What rum was left was put away for medicinal purposes, and the population settled in for the long winter.

~ Chapter Seven ~

The Long Hard Winter

As was typical of the Indian Islands area, we were experiencing winter's worst conditions by the time Christmas ended. The level grasslands and marshes were very bleak and exposed. There were no hills or trees to provide shelter from the elements. The snow would drift and level off at the tops of the fences and higher. The surrounding beaches became an endless circle of ballycadders. Sometimes the tickle would freeze over and provide safe travel by foot. More often, though, it was choked with thick slob ice or northern ice which made travel difficult and at times, impossible.

Stag Harbour Run and Hamilton Sound stretches were most inhospitable and very rarely was it safe to cross in winter. For all practical purposes the Islands were virtually isolated from January until May. The mail got through but seldom on schedule. Our mail was brought from Lewisporte overland to Boyd`s Cove, from there it was taken to Fogo Island, with ours having to go to Stag Harbour, the nearest point to the Islands.

To go to Stag Harbour in the winter was a major accomplishment, even though it was only three miles away. Contact with the outside world was maintained by wireless telegraphy — there was no telephone service then. Lucky were the people who kept healthy and well.

The nearest doctor was at Fogo, the nearest hospital was in Twillingate. To make matters worse, both these communities existed in their own isolation as both were also on islands.

Some of the patent medicines in use were Beef Iron & Wine, Brick's Tasteless, Friar's Balsam, Minard's Linament, Radway's Ready Relief, Carters Little Liver Pills, Aspirin And Cod Liver Oil. Serious illness meant untold suffering and often certain death.

Most years, people had adequate supplies of the basic foodstuffs which they shared with each other. There were always some families who, through illness or otherwise, could not provide for themselves. There was no social assistance plan in place. The more fortunate shared freely with their less fortunate neighbours.

The chief indoor activities during the winter were reading books, which were passed from house to house, card playing, and knitting twine for cod trap repairs and for new traps. Mat hooking was done mainly by women as was the never-ending chores of knitting wool socks, sweaters and mitts. All of the women could knit. My mother was the fastest knitter I ever saw. If a poll were taken I believe it would have confirmed her as the champion knitter. Her steel knitting needles moved like greased lightening.

Everyone joined in knitting twine. It might be useful for me to explain how the meshes were made to produce the netting for cod traps. The twine used was bought in the fall of the year along with the winter's food supplies. The amount to be purchased depended upon the success of the fishery that summer. On average, it would be about 200 pounds. The twine was bought in bundles of 50 pounds, made up of 10 rands of 5 pounds each. The twine was transferred to a needle for knitting. To transfer the twine from the rand to the needle was a tricky process, because the twine was easily tangled. To prevent this entanglement, one person could hold the rand over his or her arms. A second person would roll the twine in a ball. Similar to rolling a wool into a ball from the skein. This operation required the effort of two people. To streamline this operation, "the whiz whaz" was invented. It was a gadget of genius, made of wood in the shape of an inverted cone.

The rand of twine was placed over the whiz what and the top of the cone was attached to the ceiling. It was generally placed in an out of the way corner attached to the ceiling by a swivel. The end of the twine was brought through an eye screwed into the wall. It was then transferred to the needle with little possibility of it tangling. Every house had a whiz whaz.

The knitting began by using an anchor on the wall with a suitable size card. A two inch card would make a four inch mesh. A three inch card would make a six inch mesh, and so on. The twine was brought around the card and tied in what was commonly called a twine knot. It was a non-slip knot. Twine was knitted in amounts called leaves, a leaf being a definite length and width

Most men were handy with wood tools. My father was no different. He used to build boats and repair old ones. Logs and timber for this work were procured from across the bay in the fall. Smaller boats could be built in the shed. Larger boats were built outside. Temporary shelter was erected to offer some protection from the biting wind and frost. Tools were kept sharp by grinding them on a large grindstone. I often turned the wheel while my father held and sharpened the tools. The tools were the hand variety, since we had no electricity. Common tools were single and double bit axes, hammers and malls, chisels, spoke shaves, augers and bits and gimblets. Various size gimblets were used to drill holes for the planking nails. Drilling the hole eliminated splits in the wood. When a plank was being nailed to the timbers, two people were required. My father, who did the nailing, held the end he was nailing. I would hold the other end of the plank until it was all nailed in place.

The timbers, knee-like pieces from the roots of large trees, were cut into shape with an axe, draw-knife and/or plane. The logs were turned into plank by a large pit saw. A pit saw is about eight feet in length and ten inches wide. To use it, a scaffold called a pit is constructed at a height of about ten feet. The log is placed in the scaffold where one sawer is located, the other sawyer is on the ground. When the log is suitably marked, the sawing begins. The man on the top drags the saw up while the man on the ground drags the saw down. By alternately lifting the saw and dragging it back down, the planks are cut from the log. This is back-breaking work and is not recommended for weak people.

Enormous amounts of energy and time were spent in keeping warm. The provision of wood, which was the chief source of fuel, was very time consuming. Depending upon the size and length, somewhere between seven hundred to one thousands sticks of wood were needed for a year. Three weeks to a month were spent in cutting wood and hauling it to the beach. In our case, it was to the beach at Rocky Point. Under ideal conditions, it would take a couple of weeks to get it moved to the Island by boat. It was then stacked in a wood pile at the rear of the house. It had to be sawn into 16 inch junks and a great portion of it had to be cleaved. Much of it was left outdoors to dry and later stored in the woodshed. During the winter it was brought to the woodbox in the kitchen. A lot of time was spent in the provision of heat for the house. Add to this the many days and weeks spent by the women making quilts and knitting inner and outer wear for all members of the family. It is clear then that one of our chief pre-occupations was keeping warm.

Unless the bay was completely frozen over, wind and tide action would cause open water on one side or other of the island. Where there was water, salt water ducks could generally be found. Sometimes when hunting, we used to get a shot in the water. More times we had to shoot on the wing. The best time for this was just at daybreak when the ducks started to fly ashore to eat. The little protruding points of land were the best places. Common gunning points were, Eastern Point, WigWam Point, Quarry Point, Shoal Point, Blundon`s Point and the Big Head.

Possession of the prime places was hotly contested. Sometimes people would be on the points hours before sunrise. Gazers (blinds) would be built out of chunks of ice and snow, chest high, with holes to see through. As many as four or five or six people might occupy one blind. Muzzle loading guns were in general use. If a single bird came by, one person shot. Dead ducks were retrieved from the water by a small boat which was kept nearby for this purpose.

If ducks were plentiful, sometimes as many as 20 or 30 would be killed. At the end of the morning`s shooting, around 8 a.m., the birds were shared and the hunters went home.

Sharing was done by the John King process. I don't know the derivation of the term. It was called John Kinging the birds. If there were six gunners, one person would share the birds in six lots. Very often there were unequal lots. For instance, if there were 22 birds shot, four men would get four birds each and two men would get only three birds. When the birds were allotted in six lots, another person would turn his back to the birds and he would John King them. He would assign a lot which he could not see to each of the six gunners. This process eliminated any cause of disagreement. It was as fair for one as for the other.

Despite the chores which we had to do, there was still time for fun. If we had a lot of cold, frosty weather and little snow, the big pond was a great place to skate. Most of us used skates which were locally made, a wooden stock fashioned in the shape of a foot, and an old file inserted in a notch in the wood which was used as the blade. The skates were tied to your boots with a string. They often slipped off and were a bit of a nuisance. Bought skates were available in St. John's and gradually were brought to the island. The skates I remember were club skates. A club pattern was on the base and I presume that's how they got the name. These were equipped with adjustable clips which clipped onto the soles of our boots. These made skating easier.

We played a game similar to hockey. Frozen horse manure made a good puck. Sticks were fashioned out of wood. Some fellows could really skate and stick handle, but I was never much good at it. The boys who were good ballplayers were also good skaters. I believe the Penny boys could have made the major leagues as they were very athletic.

The winter provided what nature denied us- hills made of snow. The highest banks always occurred between our house and George Hynes house, about a hundred yard distance. Sometimes after school, but mainly after our lessons were done at night, we went sliding. We used small sleighs and hand-slides. We would sometimes ride as far as 60 to 70 yards. This was great fun and a great way to meet girls, who also enjoyed this rough and tumble sport.

There was a plentiful supply of good fertile soil on our island. Most families grew more vegetables than they could consume and sold the excess on Fogo Island and Change Islands. Farming ranked second only to the fishery in economic importance. While it was back breaking work, some of my most pleasant memories are the days I spent with my father and mother sowing the seed in the spring and harvesting the crop in the fall.

Barn manure, a product of our horse, sheep, goats and hens was our main source of fertilizer. This was supplemented by rotten sea weed (kelp) which was harvested from the beaches the previous year. Both of these fertilizers were used at planting time.

Caplin or cod puddings were used as an additional nutrient at trenching time, when the seeds were first breaking through the ground.

The horse and cart were used to haul the manure, kelp and fish to the gardens. When our horse, Queen, died we lost not only our means of transport but considerable source of manure. A wheelbarrow replaced the cart and more kelp replaced the horse`s contribution to the manure.

Pushing a wheelbarrow full of kelp or caplin over a sandy beach and a bumpy road to the garden must have been among the hardest work any human being could ever be required to perform. My father and I made hundreds of trips. He was much stronger than I was and could wheel bigger loads. Mom was never permitted to wheel the wheelbarrow, but she certainly did her share of other work in the gardens.

In an average year we would harvest about 30 barrels of potatoes and 10 barrels of turnips. Half of this was stored in the cellar for the winter and next year`s seed. The remainder was sold. Our potatoes were the minion variety. They had a rough reddish skin and were very dry. The small garden across the road was used for other vegetables such as carrot, parsnip, beet, onions, etc. My mother regarded it as her garden. My father and I helped her prepare it but she attended it herself until harvest time.

One of my responsibilities was to feed and water the animals in the barn, and keep the barn clean. I got help from my father at lambing and kidding time.

In May the sheep were sheared and turned loose to pasture. The lambs were either slaughtered for meat in the fall or kept as stock replacement. The wool was carded, spun into yarn and knit into sweaters, mitts and socks. The goats were let loose, but they either came back or were brought back every day for milking, once the kids were weaned. This was accomplished by separating the kids from the mother goat and supplementing the kid`s diet. The kids were slaughtered in the fall for meat supplements.

As was the practice in most communities, fences were erected around houses and gardens to keep animals out, not to keep them in. Docile sheep posed no problem. Goats were different. To keep them from getting through openings in fences they were equipped with yokes.

This was a triangular shaped wooden frame which was put over the neck, behind the head and horns. This arrangement was very effective in keeping the goats out. There was something devilish about goats. They weren't adverse to ramming you from behind and knocking you over. It seemed they would eat anything. Prime dried salt fish seemed to be attractive to them. Clothes, especially ladies underwear drying on the clothesline was also on their diet list. With all their faults, the two we owned kept us supplied with milk and cream.

Generally speaking, hens were kept in a yard. They were fed scraps from the kitchen and proper chicken feed. Hens are scavengers and if let loose would eat just about anything they might find on the beaches and elsewhere. Too much fish in the diet causes the egg yoke to be more reddish than yellow. Sensitive palates could detect a fishy taste, consequently hens were controlled in their own yard.

To ensure the hens didn't get through holes in the fence, they were equipped with wing sticks. This was a slender piece of wood about one foot long, half inch in diameter or square. It was arranged over the hens`s back and tied to the wings. The ends would protrude about four inches on either side of the bird. Thus unless they found a large opening they could not get through. It worked similar to the yoke on the goat. The ducks were turned loose and spent almost all of their days in the running brook adjacent to our property. I used to collect the eggs from the hens in the morning and in the evening, not that they laid twice in the same day but because their laying was staggered. I generally brought them food and they were always pleased to see me come around. The rooster however never did trust me. He guarded his harem rather aggressively, and he made sure that I wasn't about to remove any of them.

~ Chapter Eight ~

Wood Cutting

Wood for fuel and building purposes was cut in winter. There were two reasons for such scheduling. First it was a period of spare time and secondly the snow and ice were used to good advantage in hauling the wood to the land-wash.

Our favorite place was across the Hamilton Sound, a spot between Musgrave Harbour and Carmanville called Rocky Point. A large supply of spruce and fir was to be found there. To cross Hamilton Sound in winter in a small row boat was a dangerous exercise. The first opportunity after the middle of January we would make the trip. We had a camp there and it would generally be a two week trip. Harvey and Ken would cut and I would haul the wood to the beach where it was placed in neat piles.

As soon as ice conditions permitted, the skiff was launched and the first activity was to cruise the wood home. This was time consuming and hard work. The water at Rocky Point was too shallow to get the large skiff to shore so the wood had to loaded on the punt, a smaller boat. It was then floated off and loaded aboard the skiff. It would generally take about three or four hours to load the skiff. Approximately 300 pieces of wood 16 feet in length constituted a load. We would cross the bay to Indian Islands where the wood was unloaded and spelled up through the stage across the road to the back yard. If the water was rough we would have to use the punt to unload the large skiff.

My Boyhood on Indian Islands

The winter of 1937 was very harsh and severe. We were prevented from crossing to Rocky Point. Our wood cutting was confined to Fogo Island and its limited wood supply. We didn't cut as much as we needed and so had to buy some wood in the fall to carry us over the winter of 1938.

We bought two boatloads from Eli Hart of Basques Harbor, a little place near Fredericton, in the bay from Carmanville. Stormy fall weather meant we could retrieve only one load of the wood meaning we faced a shortage for the coming winter.

To supplement our supply, one day in late November, Harvey and I proceeded to Dog Bay Islands.. We moored our boat in a good harbour, protected from winds and seas, planning to stay there for four or five days.

The second day the morning broke calm and fine. We decided it was a good day to go to Basques Harbour and get the load of wood which we had purchased but could not get earlier. We quickly picked up our things, pulling in our moorings, started up the engine and departed for Basques Harbour across the Hamilton Sound. We were more than half way over when the wind came up out of the north east. We considered turning back but decided to proceed. By the time we reached the other side a full blown northeast storm was upon us. We had to scramble to save our boat. Instead of going to Basques Harbour we headed for Berry Head Harbour about three miles up the sound from Basques Harbour.

The harbour was formed by a small high island attached to the mainland by a beach. It was a snug harbour. We moored the boat, fore and aft, and retired to the cuddy. We cooked and ate supper. The wind was screaming and the rain was coming down in sheets. Though the harbor was safe, the boat bobbed about quite a bit. We slept in spurts and longed for the night to end. Morning broke but the storm had now reached such fury we could hardly tell the difference.

In the afternoon we decided to go ashore and walk down to Basques Harbor where Uncle Eli Hart lived, the man from whom we bought the firewood. It took us about three hours to walk the four mile distance. The trek took us through heavily wooded country. We were thoroughly soaked on arrival.

Uncle Eli was astonished to see us and, since his wife was visiting Gander Bay, he soon had a hot meal prepared for us. Harvey and Uncle Eli chatted all night. I listened! At about 10:30 p.m. we had a lunch and retired for the night. Uncle Eli went to the one bedroom in the winter house to which he had now moved. Harvey lay on a settle against one wall in the kitchen, and I lay on the floor on the opposite side. It being a small house we weren't that far apart. I quickly drifted fast asleep, to be awakened by the bone chilling screams coming from Uncle Eli's bedroom. I was really frightened and was afraid to enquire wether or not Harvey was awake. I moved over to get closer to him and was greatly comforted when he whispered that he was awake. He was also concerned and frightened.

Uncle Eli was obviously having a terrible nightmare. He suddenly same rushing out of the bedroom, cursing and shouting. He was trying to locate his shot gun. He hollered, "If I can find that goddamn shotgun I'll let you fellows know who is in charge."

We didn't know if he was referring to us or whether he was still dreaming. I was trembling, wondering what would happen next. Oh, to be back in the cuddy of the skiff in Berry Head Harbour!

Suddenly, Uncle Eli rushed out between us. Taking his gun from over the door he went outdoors and began searching for his axe. He found the axe and promptly began to chop at the side of the house. We were astute enough to find the gun resting by the chopping block where he had laid it when he picked up the axe.

We approached him very carefully and were relieved to no end when he appeared to be regaining his senses. He put the axe down and proceeded to his bedroom. He went to bed without saying a word and promptly fell asleep.

He arose bright and early. Not a word about the night's experience was mentioned, and we didn't raise it. Now I had heard about people being "hag-rode," troubled by nightmares, but I had never witnessed this happening. Harvey and I wondered what might have triggered the nightmare. That question was soon answered. On our arrival the previous afternoon, Uncle Eli informed us his wife had gone to Gander Bay for a couple of days. After breakfast, he informed us in a rather sad way that his wife had left him some time ago and had returned to her home in Gander Bay. His hag-ride was attributed to that.

As the morning passed, the storm abated. We were concerned about our relatives back home. It had been a terrible storm and they would certainly be worried about us. We shouldered our wood down to the landwash and left to return to our boat. As a result of the torrential rainfall, the "I`m Alone" was half full of water. We pumped her out and dried out the engine. Our bedclothes were up on the top bunk in the cuddy and were dry. We brought some dry wood onboard, started a fire in the bogey and stayed onboard the second night. We had no intention of having another night with Uncle Eli.

The next morning was bright, dry and calm. We had a breakfast of sorts, started the engine and left for Uncle Eli`s place. We loaded our wood, said our good-byes to Uncle Eli and left for home about 2:00 p.m. When we were about half way to Indian Islands we saw this boat coming towards us. It was our uncle, Art Frampton, in the Iron Duke. As we passed each other, he turned around and followed us. We suddenly realized they were searching for us. Soon we met Max Collins, Harvey`s brother-in-law, in the Joker and several other boats.

To realize we were the subject of a search hurt our pride and we completely ignored the boats and continued towards the Island. The wind was from the west. It was breezing and getting cold. The sea was still rough around the Island from the effects of the Northeaster. It would be too dangerous to go down to where we lived. We decided to anchor our boat at the fall anchorage in Clay Island Tickle. This is a protected place on the west end of our Island. We moored the I'm Alone, went ashore in the punt, hauled it out of the water and walked home. At every house we passed on the way people rushed out. They were so glad we were safe and wondered who had found us. Here were our friends exhibiting every kindness known to them, but because our pride was hurt we were blind to it. When we arrived at our house, Harvey was livid. He laid down the law. Never again were they to send a search party for us, no matter what. We were quite capable of looking after ourselves. Mother and his wife, Vera, tried to explain the reason for the search, but they never got to first base.

However, my father, who said nothing up to this point said, "Just a damn minute now. When you fellows left here, four days ago, you said you were going to Dog Bay Islands. Well, shortly after you left, Max Collins went to Dog Bay (Horwood) to buy lumber. He saw your boat moored in the harbour at Dog Bay Islands. He was caught in the storm at Horwood, but got away yesterday and reached home. When they passed by Dog Islands your boat was no longer there. When they came home you weren't here either. Naturally they came to inquire if we knew anything about you. We didn't. It was my decision, based on these facts, to start the search for you, and you should be damned pleased I did."

That took the wind out of our sails. We had to swallow our pride and apologize to the extent we could. It was all soon forgotten because there was a wedding that night. Harvey Downer got married to Bess Collins, no relation. The wedding was in the school house. There was lots of home-brew and moonshine. Frank Saunders provided according music. I soon forgot the storm and Uncle Eli Hart. I was too young to drink but I could dance. Everybody had a good time.

~ Chapter Nine ~

The Big Cod Fish Haul

One winter, my brother Harvey and I made a very large cod-trap. Prior to starting fishing in the spring we bought a small schooner, named the Eastern Lilly. She was about 50 tons and in addition to all of the sails she was also equipped with a 12 hp diesel engine. She could carry 600 quintals of salt bulk cured codfish. It was the summer that Uncle Allan Sheppard, Stanley Kinden and Frank Saunders fished with us as share-men.

We fished at home from the Island until mid-July when the fish struck off. At that time we moved our big cod trap to the bight between Cape Fogo, North Bill and Pigeon Island Tilting. We sailed the Eastern Lilly to Sandy Cove, just north of Tilting, to be used as a floating stage and living quarters. Crews in smaller boats used Tilting, which was a much better harbour. We couldn't go there because the water was too shallow to anchor our schooner.

The large trap produced enough fish to make the trip successful. By the first week in August the fish were becoming scarce. Some people removed their traps from the water but we decided to leave the big trap for a few more days. Several other crews who had traps in the same area also left them in the water in the event there might be another run of fish. On Friday, the fish slacked off and on Saturday we had only a couple of quintals. We returned to the Eastern Lilly, split our fish, salted it and left to return to the island around 3:00 p.m.

Most other crews returned home that day as well. On our way to Indian Islands we had to cross the bight where our trap was set and naturally, we passed close to it. As we approached the trap we noticed what looked like a piece of submerged ice in it. We turned around the skiff and stopped the motor, and to our surprise and glee found the trap was full of fish. We immediately set about hauling up the doors and cut the linnet to the V`s holding the fish in front of us and keeping them from escaping. I was directed to get in the punt and keep the back head rope from sinking, and the remainder of the crew undertook the back-breaking task of "drying-up" the fish. Finally it was all dry and reached all across the back of the trap. The fish were the largest we had seen all summer.

The wind was calm and there was very little movement in the water. We loaded the I`m Alone with 25 quintals, and we also filled two 25 quintal cod-bags and secured them. This made a total of 75 quintals and you could scarcely miss it., the trap was so full. We raised signals on our mast to attract other fishermen, but not a boat was to be seen. The people from Indian Islands and Seldom had all returned home and the people from Tilting did not bother to haul their traps in the evening as there had been few fish in the morning.

On the basis of the depth of the trap and the measurement of the back and sides, I calculate that the trap was holding anywhere from 800 to 900 quintals of fish. We debated the idea of sewing up the door of the trap to prevent the fish from escaping but in the end we decided against it because of the inherent danger in the event of a storm. Sadly we let the trap down. We returned to our schooner, and as soon as the I`m Alone was emptied we returned for another load. We secured three loads, which included the two cod bags. Crews from Sandy Cove and Tilting on learning of our success, immediately left to haul their traps. Most of them were also successful and experienced unusually big hauls of fish. Monday morning we hauled the trap again and we had two boat loads of fish, most of which were injured or dead.

By Tuesday, that scull of fish had passed by and after another week had passed the traps were removed from the water. We often wondered what might have happened had we sewn the doors to our trap. My father`s view was that all of the fish would have died and we possibly could not have removed it before it had decomposed. We will never know!

~ Chapter Ten ~

The Demon of Blundon's Island

While the chief means of transportation to and from Indian Islands was by boat there was a road which extended the whole length of the island. The road ran along the beach with houses built on the land side with the exception of Walt Penney, Solomon Collins and Jim Collins whose homes were built on protruding jibs of land on the landwash side. There were no street lights. Walking the road at night was quite hazardous. Horses, sheep and goats used the same road and without a light one could easily collide with these animals. Not a pleasant experience in the dark! Because of this, flashlights were used for moving around at night. These were available in two, three and even five cell lengths, meaning they were powered in 2, 3 or 5 size D batteries. These are still available today. I was lucky enough to own a three cell light. With new batteries, it could throw a light beam half a mile.

One night late in the fall, I was visiting my good friend, Art Penney, at his house, some distance down the road from where I lived. I left his house about 10 p.m. to return home. The gate to our front garden was the swinging type. A heavy weight such as a rock or a piece of anchor chain was attached to one end of a rope. The other end was directed through a pulley and then attached to the gate. When the gate was pushed open the weight was lifted off the ground. When one passed through the gate the weight of the suspended chain or rock automatically closed the gate. The gate opened to the inside so you could run at the gate from the outside forcing it open without stopping and we knew the gate would close behind us. It came in handy if you were being chased by a ghost or a man with no head. At night, ghosts and other types were supposed to be lurking around every corner and especially in Walt Penney's house, which was now unoccupied. Most nights I hit the gate going full speed, never looking back until I had the back porch door open. On this particular night I hesitated after passing through the gate and shone my light up and down the road. I saw nothing unusual other than a few sheep chewing their cud. I then directed the beam of light across the Tickle in the direction of Blundon's Island. To my surprise a light beam shone back at me. I turned my light off and the other light went out. It mirrored every move I made. This night was particularly calm with just a draft of wind from the southeast. Conditions were perfect for the transmission of light and sound.

I called out and my call was answered. At first I thought it was my echo, but it soon proved otherwise. There was no reason for people to be on Blundon's Island, so I thought here is another ghost! I rushed to the house and began explaining to my parents who were getting ready to retire for the night. My face must have exhibited my terrible inner shock or fear, and my mother became concerned and tried to console me. My father made little of it and suggested we all go to bed.. He thought this was just another case of my imagination. I said what I was telling them was for real and after much persuasion my father put on his boots and came outside with me. I was determined to prove it to him

In the stillness of that dark and eerie night both my father and I walked out to the gate, and from the exact spot where I was standing before, I shone my light towards Blundon's Island. Would you believe, there was no response. I tried three or four times and still no response. I called out several times and except for my echo no voice called back. My father said, "Alright my son, let's go in." My heart sank in my boots. As we walked towards the house I kept flashing my light and just as we were about to go inside, I got a response. "Hey, Pop, Pop, there it is, look!" He turned just in time to see the light. We both returned to the gate and the light beams and calls were again responded to. It was getting late at night and by some of

My Boyhood on Indian Islands

the sounds and actions we received my father came to the conclusion that someone was in some trouble over on the island. My brother Harvey and Ken were in the lumber woods at Millertown and so could not assist us and our boat had been hauled upon the beach for the winter.

Pearce Sheppard's boat, however, was still in the water. My father decided to go up the road and inform Pearce of the situation and perhaps Pearce would agree to take his boat out to investigate. I went along with him to Pearce's house. Pearce agreed to go. His son, Cyril, was my age and he came with us. We launched the small punt and rowed out to their big skiff which was anchored on the collar. We slipped the collar. Cyril started the engine and we were on our way to Blundon's Island. As you can see from the map of Indian Island, Blundon's Island is separated from West Indian Island by a small tickle of water. We could go through it at high tide but the tide was out. When we arrived at the tickle, we stopped the engine and listened. With the exception of the water lapping the rocks, not a sound could be heard. We shone our lights around and called out quite loudly, but there was no response. We waited several minutes and then father and Pearce decided to return home.We came back, put the boat on the collar, and were rowing towards shore in the small punt when the light reappeared. We called out and our calls were answered. but it was too far for the transmission of intelligent information to Blundon's Island Tickle.

When we arrived for the second time there was no light to be seen and no sound to be heard. By this time our fathers were beginning to show their displeasure. I was convinced by this time that the object of our search was no ghost. Instead of returning to the collar, the men decided to go out and around Blundon's Island and up in the bight. When we had proceeded about half way up to the bottom of the bight, the beam of my light picked up a large white boat. I kept my light shining on it and we steered in her direction. At last we were close by. Cyril stopped the engine and we proceeded very carefully because the water was shallow. The boat was high aground, there were no people to be seen. The boat had a housing over its midships. It was similar to the passenger boats which were used to take people to and from Lewisporte or to the hospital. Subsequently, we boarded the boat. Down below were three men who appeared to be asleep. On futher and close examination it was discovered they had been drinking because empty bottles were on the floor. My father and Pearce were big able and strong men, and now they were mad. The men on the boat were brought to their senses to the extent that it was possible. They seemed to be content in their condition, so we left and returned home. The boat was from Musgrave Harbour. The men who owned it and the school inspector will remain nameless for obvious reasons. The next morning when we arose the tide was high and the boat was gone. Had I failed to convince my father and had we not gone back to Blundon`s Island the second time, another ghost story would have been born and still being told.

~ Chapter Eleven ~

Survival

For those of us who lived on Indian Islands, survival was keeping body and soul together. To survive, one had to provide for oneself. Fish were caught and eaten fresh, in season. Winter supplies were preserved by salting. Vegetables were grown in the fields, there was no need for anyone to be without. Goats and hens were suppliers of meat, milk and eggs. Other meats were provided by sheep and pigs supplemented by seals and birds. To get seals and birds required great hunting skills. You either developed these skills and were successful, or you did without. I received good training from my father and older brothers. With much practice I became a good bird hunter. I was a crack shot with rifle and shot gun.

Our dependence on sea birds was equaled only by the Labrador natives` dependence on seal and caribou. The chief species which we hunted were eider ducks, turrs, tickleaces, bowks (great shearwater) and partridge (ptarmigan), to name a few.

I hunted several times with Harvey and Ken, but only if it was convenient for them. They both liked to shoot and my job was to look after the boat and retrieve dead and wounded birds. If a third party went with them I was not permitted to go. One such morning was in the spring of the year when I was nine years old. The teacher, who was boarding with us, decided to go with them, and while I was out of bed at 3:00

a.m. they wouldn't take me. I raised a bit of cane and father and mother reluctantly let me take the small punt provided I promised not to go too far. I agreed and rowed over between Blundon`s Island and Shoal Point. I made one of my better shots that morning. A flock of hounds (old squaw) flew by me and I had my first shot for the morning. The flock contained about 25 to 30 birds and when I shot the whole damned works (all of them) dropped in the water. It was only an instant before most of them resumed flight again, but I had shot six. I considered that as one of my better wing shots. I wasn't aware until after that this was a common trait for sea birds. They were great followers and if one landed or fell they all followed.

That morning I was using my fathers 7/8" muzzle loader. The gun was about 6 feet long and quite heavy. I couldn't keep it to my shoulder for any great period of time. It was up and shoot so to speak. The gun was convenient for hunting from a boat because it was laid down while you were moving around. If you were hunting on land it was really too heavy to carry any distance. If it was loaded properly and you shot straight success was assured. An average load would be three fingers of black powder as measured on the rod. A wad of oakum was rammed in place. Two fingers of number 4 shot followed with another wad of oakum on top of it. The shot wad was just tapped down, merely used to keep the shot running out of the barrel, in the event the gun was not properly elevated.

Harvey used a smaller 3/4" bore muzzle loader, a much lighter gun. Ken used a brand new 12 gauge Richardson and Harrison, with a 36" barrel. I was never permitted to use that, but I did on the day when I spotted a partridge from the school window one afternoon in November.

Snow had fallen on two or three occasions and partridge had started to assume their white winter plumage. Sometimes in the fall of the year the snow would melt and the white partridge stood out against the colourful fall background. Such was the scenario when I looked out through the school window about half way through the afternoon class. A covey of 10-12 birds could be seen on a barren behind our house, which was just up the road from the school. I can visualize them now. They looked as big as geese. I didn't do much work for the rest of the afternoon, I was so anxious to get out and go after these birds. I wasn't sure if any of my friends had seen the birds, but as soon as school closed it was clear that they had.

Art Penney took off like a scaled cat, Cyril Sheppard, who lived up the road, took off in that direction with similar intent. Our house was closer to the school so I reached home quickly. I rushed in the door, grabbed the first gun I saw, which was my brother's 12 gauge, took three or four shells from the ammunition bag and hurried across the garden towards the barren where the partridge were.

I could see Art Penney converging on the barren from the east and Cyril Sheppard coming from the opposite direction. I had the advantage of being closer to the birds, but there was no time to lose. To ensure I didn't flush the birds before they were in range, I crawled the last 50 yards on my belly. When I finally reached a little clump of bushes I knew I was close enough. The trouble was my heart was beating about 200 times per minute from excitement and exhaustion. As soon as I could steady myself, I flushed the birds, took aim and fired. Three partridges hit the barren, two dead and one wounded. Art and Cyril turned and went home, and I gave chase after the wounded bird. Anyone who has ever endeavored to retrieve a wounded partridge will know how difficult it can be. Finally, in a desperation move, I fell down and grabbed the bird. I picked up the other two and returned home, only to find the stock of the gun was broken. It must have occurred when I tripped and fell. Thanks to my mother I'm still alive. My brother Ken wanted to kill me.

On another occasion, one year later, I was hunting partridge on Perry's Island. The big marsh on the island was a great place for birds. However, on this day the birds were scarce, and the few I did see were very wild. I didn't use a dog so the hunt was rather strenuous and at best uncertain. I was heading back to my boat to go home when I noticed a large flock of partridge coming across from Change Islands. They landed on the highest part of the marsh about three gunshots away from me. The flock contained about 50 birds which would be at least 5 or 6 coveys.

On this day I was using the big muzzle loader. I had the powder horn and shot bag on my back. I was wishing I had a breech loader because if I could get close enough I might get two shots. I would be limited to one shot with the muzzle loader.

I began to stalk the birds. They were very uneasy and before I could get close they took flight. They flew back in the direction they'd come from and were over the water in Stag Harbour Run, when they suddenly reversed direction and came back. Instead of coming to the open marsh, however, this time they landed in the tuckamore which formed a hedge around the marsh where it met the beach. This tuckamore was little more than waist high but was very dense. My spirits lifted as I knew now I had a good chance to get in range. I couldn't see the birds but I knew where they were. It was getting late in the afternoon so I hurried across the bog until I came to the edge of the tuckamore. I stopped and, after taking a few deep breaths, I entered the brush with my thumb on the cock of the gun, ready for action. When I knew I was close enough I made some noise by kicking the bushes and shouting. The birds started to flush but chiefly in ones and twos at a time. I wanted more before I shot. Eventually the main body of birds came up and I picked my birds and fired. When the smoke cleared and the birds that got away disappeared out of sight, I searched for the birds I had killed. I picked up five. Not a bad shot for partridge. I returned across the marsh to my boat and arrived home just as darkness was setting in.

Hunting at sea was done from an open boat, which we always referred to as a punt. Since we had no engines we rowed or, if the wind cooperated, we used a small sail. Very often we would row several miles to arrive at our destination just at the break of dawn when the birds were most active. Stephen Crane`s story "The Open Boat" was based on his personal experience. He said, " Rowing a boat was not an amusement. It was a diabolical punishment. Even a genius of mental aberrations could never conclude that it was anything but a horror to the muscles and a crime to the back."

That statement was based on his one experience when he was adrift and lost in an open boat overnight. I often wonder what he would have said if he had been required to row a boat for a living. The boats we used were built for our conditions and they were typically 14 feet long and 4 feet wide, with a sturdy bow and square counter. There were two rowing positions, one fore and one aft. The fore seat had a three inch hole in the center for the sail mast. This presented a real problem to your rear end when rowing. Each man used two oars, referred to as paddles. The oars were held in place on the rollicks of the gunwales by a rope called a withe which fitted over the oar and the rollick "tole pin." In winter time, slob haulers replaced paddles for maneuvering through heavy slob ice. I wonder what Crane would have written had he been required to chase young seals in the water all day. My arms and chest are still strong because of it. I can`t say the same for my back. The young people today are missing out on the real enjoyment of rowing a punt.

~ Chapter Twelve ~

Partridgeberry Picking on Copper Island

Copper Island lies in the mouth of the bay, about five miles south of the southern head of Fogo Island. Relatively speaking, it is a very high island with the granite cliffs dropping perpendicular to the sea. There is only one place on the southwest corner where it's possible to land in a small boat. The island contains some trees but is mainly barren land, a great place for partridgeberries. It is also a great place for puffins who nest there in the thousands.

Some years we would visit the island to kill some puffins. It was a great sport. Most birds, like ducks and scotters, fly at speeds of about 40 mph. Puffins coming down from these cliffs were clipping along at 80 or 90 mph and they posed a real challenge on the wing. After a shot or two we would get used to the speed and make corrections for it. It was the only bird where you would have to aim just ahead of its head in order to knock it down. Other birds you could shoot for their heads and if you shot straight they would fall every time.

My father used to tell stories about some of his trips to the island in his younger years. In addition to shooting puffins, they would also pick substantial quantities of partridge berries, which were quite plentiful.

This particular year the berries were quite plentiful and large. In no time they all had all of their containers filled and were heading back to the boat when they came upon this extra large berry.

They continued to the boat and put their containers onboard and returned to fetch this large berry. It was much too large to put in a bucket, so they decided to roll the berry across the barrens to the cliff above the boat. They took their time because they didn't want to break the outer skin and lose the juice. Upon reaching the top of the cliff above the boat they proceeded to construct a par-buckel to lower the berry down to the boat. The boat was properly positioned underneath the cliff and the par-buckel, made of ropes gathered from the boat, was made ready. The huge berry was positioned between the ropes and they proceeded to lower it down.

Everything was going fine until the berry was just about in the boat. Right at that moment an unexpected swell lifted the boat and the berry hit the tole pin in the gunwale. The berry slipped out of the par-buckle and burst. Father said the boat was almost swamped but fortunately most of the juice went overboard. They had to clean the boat and paint her red on the inside to get rid of the stains. He also claimed that the water around Copper Island remained red in color until a northeast storm later in the fall mixed it up.

~ Chapter Thirteen ~

The Fall of the Year

Just as spring was a period of intense and exciting activity in preparation for summer, fall was a time of consolidation and rather frantic preparation for winter. The new teacher arrived on the coastal boat. The wharf was crowded with people seeking a first glimpse of him or her as they arrived in the mailboat from the ship anchored in the tickle. School was reopened and new books were distributed.

The summer catch of fish was prepared for the market. The harvesting of fruits and vegetables began. Food was stored away for the winter, wood to heat our houses was brought to the Island. Boats were pulled from the water. People relocated from the summer back kitchens to the warmer parts of the house. Stages and stage heads were battened down or taken ashore.

Every precautionary measure was taken to deal with the savagery and fury of the northeast winds. However, not all was doom and gloom. It was a time for feasting. I'll never forget the aroma of the great scoffs my mother used to cook. At potato digging time she would leave the garden early, about mid-afternoon, her apron full of fresh potatoes, turnips, carrot and cabbage. Cooked with salt beef and a fresh duck or two with gravy, you had an evening meal fit for a king. Bakeapple tarts and tea made from pure well water followed. It was the time of the year when animals were rounded up. Those excess to breeding needs were slaughtered and prepared for winter.

Yearling lambs, kids and pigs were the unfortunate ones. In addition to the meat which they provided, pigs were of great interest to the boys. The killing of a pig always attracted boys as their bladders were used for footballs so we had to make sure it was retrieved. The bladders were cleaned and placed in brine, generally from the family beef barrel, where it stayed until it had toughened. This would normally take two weeks. It was then removed from the brine, washed again and cleaned. The next process was to have your mother knit or make a suitable cover. It was then inflated and used for a football. The one difference between it and the regular ball was in weight. It was much lighter. Sometimes when it was blowing hard and the ball was kicked in the air, it blew off the island. Many were lost that way.

In addition to kick football, we also played rounders, a game very similar to baseball. The balls were made of solid rubber or other suitable material, generally covered with cloth. The bats were made of tough spruce or birch wood, flattened on one side. This made hitting easier. Rounders differed from baseball, as we know it today, in that the pitcher didn't try to strike the batter out. Instead, the batter was encouraged to hit the ball and put it in play. If it was a fly ball and was caught by a fielder, the batter was out. If it was a ground ball, the fielder who fielded the ball would aim and throw the ball at the runner. If the runner was hit before he reached base, the runner was out. Three outs and the fielders took turn at bat. The balls would become very hard when they were wet and frozen, consequently many runners who were hit with the ball still carry their bumps.

~ Chapter Fourteen ~

How to Track an Owl

Elijah Collins, who lived on the point near where my father was born, used to tell Arthur Penney and me stories about his life. No doubt some were true, others were a product of his vivid imagination, or were just tall tales. He wasn't a relation of ours but we always called him Uncle Lija. Art and I dropped into his store after school one day in winter. Uncle Lija was building a boat and hanging over the workbench was a large snowy owl. We were fascinated with the large bird and wondered how he managed to get it because owls were notoriously difficult to hunt.

Uncle Lija put down his tools and proceeded to tell us. He said that owl had been here all one winter and most mornings could be seen on the big rock. The rock was a huge boulder about twenty feet in diameter and was perched on top of a shoal in front of Uncle Lija`s premises. It was about 150 yards off from his stage head. In those days, people shot at everything that could fly and the owl was hunted, even though it was never eaten, it being a bird of prey. He said how he had tried every trick in the book but could never get in range of the bird. The owl seemed to be able to measure the distance between itself and the hunter and knew when to take flight.

Uncle Liga said he'd read an article in the Family Herald on how to hunt owls. It suggested that calling out to the owl and telling it where you were headed and then the owl would become relaxed. Most often the hunter could then walk close enough to shoot it.

This morning, he said, he took his kerosene oil can and pretended he was going across the tickle to Nick Perry`s for some oil. He called out and told the owl what he proposed to do. In a few minutes he started walking towards Nick`s store in the direction which would keep him well clear of the owl. As he progressed, he very gradually changed direction but never walked directly towards the bird. The owl was completely relaxed and very soon Uncle Lija was in range. He shot the owl. Now, he said, there`s a lesson for you. If you follow these instructions you will never fail. We both doubted the validity of the story, but we resolved to follow his advice if we ever saw an owl.

One year a fellow named Edgar Boland was teaching on our island in our school. He boarded with us. Edgar was from now resettled Pinchard`s Island and I`m told he is still living in retirement at Badger`s Quay. Coming from an island like ourselves, Edgar was very familiar with hunting techniques, and he was not adverse to brag about what a good shot he was. He and I hunted several times, and I would have to say he was a good shot and a good sport.

My brother Harvey and his wife, Vera, and children lived in an extension to our house. They had their own back and front entrance. Vera was pregnant this year and her sister`s daughter, Jessie Penney, used to help her out doing chores around the house. Edgar thought a lot of Jessie and was making all the moves to court her. He played many tricks on Jessie and she didn't seem to object to it. One day in October, Edgar and I went up on Perry`s Island marsh to hunt partridge. It was on a Saturday. We hunted all day and had no luck. On our return across the marsh to where we had landed our boat, we spotted a large owl. He was perched on the highest knob he could find and could see everything that moved in any direction. Edgar and I knew we would never get close enough to shoot at it. It was then that Uncle Lija`s story came to mind. I said, "Boland, I know how to get that owl if you will help me." He agreed, and I planned the strategy. I instructed him to keep a long distance from the owl and walk past it until the owl was just about in line between us, "When you get there, keep walking about and calling, saying you are going back across the tickle. In that way you should get the owl's attention and I will stalk up from behind and shoot it."

Edgar was sure that I was cracking up after a long day on the marsh, but he agreed to do it because he was walking towards the boat anyway. When he reached the appointed place he did what I told him to do. I could tell he had the owl's attention. I kept on walking in the same direction at a bit of an angle to the bird on a path which would take me close enough to shoot it. When I arrived at about 50 yards from the bird I shot it. It was the first and last owl I ever shot, and I still feel sad about it. I was going to leave the noble bird where it was, but Edgar wanted it to take home. He brought it to the boat and we left for our Island. On arrival Edgar brought the bird to our house and after mother and father saw it, he took it outside and hung it in the store. After supper we both went over to Harvey's house and before too long Jessie arrived.

Edgar thought a good trick to play on Jessie would be to hang the owl over the outside door of Harvey's house at a level where it would hit her face when she opened the door. He confided in me and left the house to get the owl. When he had the owl placed in the proper position outside the door he knocked on the door. This was supposed to get our attention inside and I was to suggest that Jessie answer the knock to see who it might be. But as quick as a flash Vera was on her feet and on the way to answer the knock on the door. When she opened it, the owl met her square in the face. She was eight month's pregnant and damned near collapsed. I ran to get my mother to come out and she brought Vera around with cold water. Edgar witnessed the whole thing from around the corner of the shed and was he ever startled when he saw what had happened. Vera drank some ginger wine and when she had completely recovered we all had a laugh, but to tell the truth Vera didn't think it was very funny.

~ Chapter Fifteen ~

The Night That Horwood's Boom Burst

My brother Harvey`s family was growing and it was necessary for him to build an extension on his house. This would require some lumber so one day in September he and my father and I set out for Gander Bay. Cash was difficult to find so Harvey reasoned that he might be able to barter some fish for lumber. We decided to go to Frank Saunders at Clarke`s Head, a businessman who also owned a sawmill. We had no trouble arranging a deal. Mr. Saunders took our fish and we selected our lumber, which we proposed to load the next day and then return home.

The water is very shallow in Gander Bay, so we decided to move our boat away from the pier. We moored our boat at the end of a salmon net which Uncle Ben Gillingham was fishing. Uncle Ben was a good friend of my father`s, so we were invited ashore to his house for supper. We enjoyed our meal and my father and Harvey played cards with Uncle Ben and his son, Nath, until 11:00 p.m. when we returned to our boat. We had planned an early rise, but we were awakened before our scheduled time by Uncle Ben coming aboard our boat.

He said, "I thought I should awaken you because Horwood`s boom up in the Gut burst during the night and there are lots of logs drifting down the bay." He said, "I figured you might be interested in getting some."

The mere mention of lots of logs was enough to send an Indian Islander into a state of tizziness. We were quickly out of our bunks, half-dressed and without breakfast we hauled in our anchor and left in search of logs. Just about five miles out of the bay we hit the main patch, as it were. Thousands of logs were adrift. We had lots of rope onboard and as we selected the best logs we tied them together. A fairly brisk wind was blowing from the west. Coupled with the effect of the tide, which was also running out the bay, we were drifting fairly quickly and soon were out to Gander Bay Islands, about half way to Indian Islands. My father suggested that we tie the 200 logs onto the punt and let it drift towards home. This we did. Then we set about to corral additional logs and boom them in a small cove on the west end of the inner Gander Bay Island. We had about 100 logs in this cove with a boom across it. Next we hauled 25 or 30 logs across the skiff and headed for home.

We didn't get far when we were intercepted by Peter Hoddinott in a rather fast boat which was owned by Horwood Lumber Company. Peter was a former Indian Islander and was now Horwood Lumber Company`s manager. He impressed upon us the fact the logs were Horwood's property and we had no right to it. He suggested we should turn around and take the logs to the boom in Gander Bay or the mill in Horwood. He offered to pay us delivery of the logs. I forget what the offer was, however, when we figured it out, it would just about cover our fuel costs only. We refused the offer and proceeded towards the Island. Peter had some harsh words to say and told us he would have us prosecuted. My father thought we would be protected by the salvage of property laws pertaining to the high seas. If so, we would be awarded at least one third the value of the salvaged material. When we arrived at Fox Island, near the west entrance to Indian Island Tickle, we found our punt and the two hundred logs tied to it. We took it in tow and arrived at our wharf just before dark. Well, you talk about excitement! The whole Island sprang into activity. We gave them all the information about where they would find the logs and of course we didn't mention the 100 logs we had in the boom on the west end of Gander Bay Island. Some people went log hunting during the night, a dangerous practice. At daylight. every boat in the community joined in the search for logs. We proceeded to Gander Bay Islands and retrieved our other logs and came home. We now had about 325 of the best logs ever cut in Gander Bay. At high tide ,we floated our logs in the mouth of the brook that ran out by our house. The brook was filled. All of the logs which were adrift were recovered by people from the Island. Some crews had only a dozen or so, while others had as many as 100. One crew had 150.

The next day Peter Hoddinott arrived on the Islands, accompanied by Const. Harvey of the Newfoundland Constabulary, who was stationed in Fogo. Peter again implored the people to take the logs to the mill at Horwood or the boom at Gander Bay. No one obliged. He made two or three offers but none were accepted. When that failed, Const. Harvey informed everyone of their rights. Having discharged that formality, he informed us we could be charged with stealing property, namely logs belonging to Horwood Lumber Company and we would be summoned to magistrate's court in due course.

Some people used their logs for wharf repairs, others merely drove nails in them, convinced the company wouldn't want any part of them because of the damage the nails would cause to the mill saws. A pretty crafty means of retaining possession! Since we had the largest number of logs and we were the first to be apprehended, quite naturally we became the chief target for the company and the law.

After a week or so had elapsed, Magistrate Beaton J. Abbott arrived from Twillingate. He and my father, a justice of the peace, were good friends and he always stayed at our house during his magisterial visits to the Island.. He came to our house and discussed the whole affair. He said the case of Horwood Lumber Company vs Harvey Frampton and Lorenzo Collins was to be heard. I was not mentioned in the suit because I was a minor.

The court was held in the school house and it was packed to the doors. I managed to sneak in as well. That was the first and last time I was ever in court and witnessed a trial.

Const. Harvey was the prosecutor and Peter Hoddinott gave testimony. Then Harvey and my father gave evidence on their own behalf. As defendants my father did most of the talking and he sure knew what he was talking about. He was an expert in the law of salvage on the high seas. When all the evidence had been heard the magistrate withdrew to his boat. On his return to the courtroom he reviewed the evidence and rendered his judgement. He found under the Law of the Sea, salvage provision, the defendants were entitled to retain one-third of the logs or be paid one-third of the value of the logs.

That was satisfactory to us and we sold our third to Peter Hoddinott. We made more money on these logs than we made fishing for all summer. Beaton J. Abbott later ran in politics and served as a minister in the Smallwood cabinet.

~ Chapter Sixteen ~

Bonfire Night

Harold Kinden, Cyril Sheppard, Art Penney and I were very close buddies and were good at playing tricks on our peers and sometimes on our elders. The night this was usually done was Bonfire Night, also known as Guy Fawkes night in memory of Fawkes, who tried to blow up the British parliament in 1605 in what was called the Gunpowder Plot.

We started planning for Bonfire Night of November 5, 1937, early in October. Three or four fires were planned by different groups for that night and ours was located up in Mary Sheppard's Bottom. Mary was Wilson Sheppard's wife and they lived in the last house up the shore. Adjacent to their property was a muddy barachois commonly referred to as a bottom and to identify this one it was called Mary's Bottom. Every bit of driftwood we could find was stored at that site and several weeks were devoted to cutting alders and any other trees we could find. As a last resort we took some wood from the family woodpiles, I think with their approval, although wood was a scarce commodity on the island.

October was harvest month and most people had removed their potatoes from the ground but turnip, carrots and cabbage were left a little longer. My father always claimed that a touch of frost improved the taste of these vegetables. As I remember, a fresh carrot or turnip eaten immediately after being pulled from the ground was a real treat, especially if taken from someone else's garden. Uncle Mark Vincent and his wife, Aunt

Emily, lived next door to the school. They were fine people and very successful gardeners. They grew a large quantity of vegetables in the garden at the rear of the house and in another smaller garden in the front. Very often during recess time Uncle Mark would come lean over the fence and engage us in conversation. You could see evidence where carrots and turnips had been removed from his garden. They blamed the school children in general but we knew that Uncle Mark figured the four of us were the main thieves. Bonfire night was about a week away when we noticed that a very large choice turnip was missing from his garden. We believed he knew we were about to steal it and we thought he had put it in the root cellar for safe keeping.

Preparations now moved into high gear and every evening after school final arrangements were put into place. It seemed that everyone on the island was involved in preparing and looking forward to the celebrations. After supper we met again and began to implement part two of the evening celebrations. Our plan was to cook a meal and invite the girls, Jessie Kinden, Gwen Collins and Louise Sheppard. Our hope was that one of the houses might be available. It turned out that Harold Kinden's parents, Uncle Ernest and Aunt Emily, had gone to Eastern Cove visiting a relative and Harold was fairly certain they would be late getting home. I arranged to get one of my mother`s pots and a piece of salt beef from the pantry barrel. We decided two days before that we were going to cook Uncle Mark's big turnip and with that in mind the four of us crept down to the landwash until we were opposite Uncle Mark's root cellar. Cyril and Art scanned the surroundings and when they made a light whistling noise it was our signal to enter the cellar. We soon located the turnip, put it in a brin bag and quickly returned to the Kinden house.

Aunt Helen Sheppard was very protective when it came to her small vegetable garden and she was next on our list. As I mentioned before we called all adults Aunt or Uncle out of respect for their age. Aunt Helen was the wife of my real and favorite Uncle Stephen. He was the type who, had he been invited, would have stolen the carrots and cabbage for us but we managed ourselves this time. Once we had our vegetables, the only thing left to get was fresh meat and I knew where to find some. Uncle George Hynes and his wife, Gertie, lived just across the running brook from our house. Two days before,

My Boyhood on Indian Islands

George had slaughtered a lamb and it was hanging in his little red store on the beach side of the road. Keeping to the landwash again the four of us managed to reach the shed. Art and Cyril went inside while Harold and I stood guard. When we gave the all clear they entered the shed and in the rush to cut a roast of lamb one whole leg became separated from the carcass. We quickly retraced our steps back to Harold`s house. Now everything was ready for bonfire night and supper. The bonfire was lit just before it became dark and lasted about two hours. We put the embers out with salt water brought up from the beach.

We then moved to part two of the evening with supper being prepared from our stolen booty. By previous agreement the girls were suppose to join us around 10:30 p.m. The meal was nearly ready by then but the girls had not arrived. After removing the roaster and pots from the stove and placing them in the warmer closet, we went searching for the girls. We didn't find them and after about half an hour we returned to the house. We could see the outside door was now open and when we entered the kitchen it was clear someone had been in the house and all our food was gone. We searched everywhere but to no avail, not a trace was found.

We were more than frustrated! We never got the girls and someone stole our stolen food. We had been tricked so we had to retaliate.

We proceeded down the road and when we passed the school and came to Uncle Mark Vincent`s house we saw that he had hauled his 14-foot punt from the water and had it turned bottom up by the side of the bank. We weren't blaming him for stealing our dinner, but we thought we would relocate his boat. We had visions of the boat in his front yard, but on surveying the situation decided to put it across his gate. He had a fancy picket fence across the front of his property and a large gate, which was hung between two massive posts. The posts were two large logs about 10 inches in diameter and about 7 feet high crowned with square tops. We satisfied ourselves that Uncle Mark and family were asleep and brought the boat from the beach to the gateway. Our plan was to put it across the gate on top of the gate posts. Just as we were about to lift one end of the boat we heard someone coming down the road. We dashed to the beach and were quite relieved when the person was Albert Collins, no relation, but a friend. We greeted him and told him of our plan and he agreed to help us. When the boat was secured across the gate we tied it in place and then went home.

The next morning at school we saw the boat was still upon the gate posts and there was no sign of Uncle Mark or any of his family. When we broke for recess the boat had been removed and Uncle Mark was leaning over his fence waiting for us. He explained that some sleeveens had taken his big turnip and he suspected the same people had played the trick with his punt. He told us it took ten men to remove the punt and no doubt just as many to put it there and was satisfied that we couldn't have done it. We told him if we ever found out who did he would be the first to know.

Art Penney retired some years ago as a captain with Marine Atlantic and I am sorry to say he has since passed away. Harold Kinden is a retired meteorological officer and resides in Moncton, New Brunswick. Cyril Sheppard retired some years ago from Canadian Overseas Telecommunications and is now living in Corner Brook.

I have another story about Bonfire Night and an incident that occurred when I was about nine. The story has to do with barrels so first let me tell you a bit more about different kinds of barrels and how important they were in our lives.

The cod liver is a by-product of the cod fish. It is retrieved during the heading and gutting procedure. This was accomplished by dropping the liver down through a hole in the splitting table, directly into a suitable container. Depending upon the price paid for fresh liver, it was sold as is or transferred to a rendering barrel. The barrels were in three sizes. The largest was called a puncheon. It was a large cask with a liquid capacity of 70 gallons and was originally used in transporting molasses from the West Indies to Newfoundland. The next smaller size was called a tierce. It had a liquid capacity of 42 gallons and was sometimes used to ship kerosene oil around the coast. The smallest container and the one most used was a barrel that could hold about 30 liquid gallons and was used to transport salted beef and pork around the coast.

When these containers were filled with livers they were left exposed to the elements out of doors, which promoted the rendering process. As the rendering took place residue from the livers sank to the bottom and some of it adhered to the sides of the barrel. The oil rose to the surface and was stored in clean barrels for shipment to the refining factories in St. John's and Carbonear. Refined oil was sold and used for medicinal purposes. It was a great source of vitamin D.

I remember drinking the unrefined product, which was generally used for curing leathers and seal skins and for illumination. When the oil was poured in a suitable container fitted with a rope wick it was often used to light the stage when fish was being split at night. It was never used in the house because it produced a terrible smell.

The barrels we used were made of wood and had to be replaced every few years due to the accumulation of cod liver residue on the sides and bottoms. The problem then was what to do with them and the easiest solution was to get rid of them by burning. The owners of the barrels would sometimes set them aside for Bonfire Night. There was little wood on the Island so getting the chance to burn those barrels and any others we could find gave us boys great pleasure.

In 1934, my father and my brother, Harvey, had purchased several new barrels, which meant they had to keep a sharp eye to ensure they weren't stolen on the nights leading up to Bonfire Night. In 1935 the cod-fishery was a failure and, like most men on the island, Harvey was obliged to find work elsewhere to provide for his family. He considered himself lucky when he found work with the Anglo Newfoundland Development Company in Millertown. Using his buck-saw and axe, he spent the fall cutting wood for the paper mill in Grand Falls. Before leaving home in September he had our trap skiff hauled from the water, and she was positioned on her side just up the beach from our wharf, by the side of the running brook which separated our premises from George Hynes property.

The night before he left Harvey came to me and charged me with the responsibility for removing the rain water from the skiff and, when Bonfire Night rolled around, to protect the new cod liver oil barrels. This responsibility which had been placed on me weighed heavily on my shoulders, and although I wasn't looking forward to Bonfire Night I went with my friends. As our fire began to fade I heard a whisper they intended to get more barrels and I suspected Harvey's new barrels were in jeopardy. I quickly ran home and asked my father what I could do, knowing all the time that because my father was crippled whatever was done would be up to me.

I eyed my father's old sealing gun which was resting on two brass hooks over the kitchen door, If I could make some noise and discharge the muzzle loader it might do the trick. My father reluctantly agreed but said I was to be careful.

The old muzzle loader was taken down and we made sure no shot remained in it, in fact I took the shot and put it back in the shot bag. Making doubly sure no shot remained I placed a couple of fingers of gun powder in the barrel and rammed it in with an oakum wad.

With the gun in hand I proceeded to the skiff which was lying on the bank next to our fishing premises. On arriving there I hid in the engine house and watched through the window.

In no time I saw four or five guys stealthily approaching the walkway to our stage, where the barrels were located. To reach the barrels they had to pass close to the side of the boat where I was hiding.

As they began to roll the barrels away, I opened the engine room door and pointed the muzzle loader towards the sky, cocked her and pulled the trigger. What a bang! "Get the hell out of here," I yelled in my best blood curdling shout, and get the hell out they quickly did.

The quickest escape route was across the running brook but little did they realize the water was high so, instead of wading, they had to swim.

I went home and told my parents, and my mother was concerned about the boys. I went back across the bridge to check on them and found them soaking wet and hanging out behind George Hynes ochre colored wood shed. They were Lender Perry from Eastern Cove, as well as Albert Collins, Art Penney and Doug Vincent who lived near us. I explained the whole situation to them and all but one of them took it as a joke.

Upon returning to his house, he reported the incident and his father visited our house the next day. As much as my father and mother tried to explain the whole situation to him he said he had no alternative but to report the incident to the authorities. He contacted Const. Harvey of the Newfoundland Constabulary at Fogo. Const. Harvey eventually arrived on the island and met with the boy's parents and my parents but nothing more came of the incident.

When my brother Harvey came home later in the fall I could gladly report nobody got his barrels!

~ *Chapter Seventeen* ~

More Memories

In 1935, our cod landings were down when compared with previous years. The law of supply and demand came into force and the price of sun-cured dried cod went up. As I recall, the price per quintal went from $2.50 to $3.50 for small and from $4.50 to $5.50 for large.

The cod trap was the chief method of catching this species. The best season for catching were the months of June and July, a time when warm temperatures and lack of refrigeration made it nigh impossible to produce a top quality product. The Spanish and Portuguese tried to deal with this problem by heavy salting the fish. With the exception of the Labrador fishery where heavy salting methods were practiced, light salting was the preferred way for the inshore product on the northeast coast of the island. Most of the fish which was produced and sold was No. 2 quality, commonly referred to as Maderia. The one constant was size: large, medium and small. Markings representing these sizes were sawed in the culler's table. While in some cases the cullers held government licenses, they were employed by the merchants and they were very much aware of that. When culling, the vast majority of the fish fell in the Maderia medium category. A considerable number fell in the small size, and a few met the requirements for large. In summer, a considerable quantity of the finished product fell into the No. 3 or West Indies category. The West Indies was the only market for No. 3.

When the fish was dried, it was stored in fish sheds. To help maintain the quality prior to shipping the inside walls of the sheds were limed, the theory being the lime would absorb the dampness in the air. While shortage in supply created greater competition among buyers, which generally should result in higher prices to the fishermen, the culling process still gave the merchant the upper hand. But in spite of everything, higher prices did benefit the fisherman.

From what I can remember about conversations with Harvey and my father, they settled their accounts with Earl and Sons at Fogo and still had about 25 quintals (112 pounds) of fairly good quality fish left in the shed. They were determined to get the best possible price for that fish and were willing to shop around. And, one evening over supper they set out a plan.

It was agreed that two good days were needed, days of westerly or northwesterly winds. One day would be needed to dry the fish and bring out what was referred to as the blossom effect, something which would improve the appearance of the fish's face. It was hoped that the culler would be favourably impressed and this would result in a better culling. The second good day was necessary for transporting the fish to market. When conditions were right, the fish was loaded on handbarrows and transported to the skiff. It was agreed that they would first test the Fisherman's Union Trading Co. at nearby Seldom. If they weren't satisfied with the cull and price, it was planned to go to Change Islands and try their luck there. Their plan was to try two quintals and if they were satisfied with the cull and price to sell the rest. If, on the other hand, the culling was unsatisfactory they would return the fish to the skiff and proceed to Change Islands.

As it turned out, they weren't satisfied and after returning the fish to the skiff they proceeded on to Change Islands where they would have two opportunities, at Earl and Sons in Fox Head Cove, and at S. Roberts down in the Main Tickle. Mr. Alex Taylor, who was Roberts' culler, seemed to be fair and the fish was sold there.

It was exactly what my mother and I expected as we discussed it over our noon day meal. Had they sold the fish at Seldom they would have been home by now. The fact they were not meant they had gone to Change Islands and would be home much later. She wondered aloud what in the world she would cook for supper because she knew they would be really hungry after all day.

We had lots of potatoes, turnips, and carrots, but she thought a change from salt beef or fish would be nice. So she said, " When you finish school this afternoon I want you to take the gun and go up along the west end of the island and see if you can get a meal of birds for supper."

I was tickled to accept the challenge. Hunting was fun and I relished the thought of being helpful to my mother. When school was dismissed, I rushed home. She had prepared a sandwich and a glass of goat's milk and I devoured it quickly.

The afternoon was closing in and I didn't have much time. I grabbed the shotgun from the rack over the kitchen door, slung the shot bag and powder horn over my neck and shoulder, and left for Mary Sheppard`s Bottom. The breeding season for plovers was long over and the birds were now concentrating in flocks, getting ready for migrating south. I searched Mary`s Bottom and went on to Cow Island. I was wearing thigh rubbers, but had difficulty getting across the tickle to Cow Island. However the water was falling and as the tide went out the sandbars were becoming exposed. Suddenly, a flock of plovers flew overhead and I followed them and determined they had landed in the bottom where Uncle Pearce Sheppard's garden was located. I quickly started in that direction. With great care, I crept within gunshot range and with just one shot I killed enough birds for supper.

When I returned to the house my mother gave me a great big kiss on my cheek. She then took a knife and a pan and we went out the lane, opened the gate, and crossed the road to the beach where we plucked and cleaned the birds.

I gathered some boughs from the flake, she scravelled some chips and put them in her apron, and we returned to the house. In no time we had a good fire going in the Waterloo stove. The birds were soon in the oven and the vegetables bubbling away in a pot on top of the stove.

As darkness was settling in, my father and Harvey arrived. When the flour, salt beef, sugar and other provisions they had purchased at Change Islands had been removed from the I`m Alone I put her on the collar. And then, over a big plate of fresh vegetables and the birds I'd shot we listened attentively to father and Harvey tell us what had happened that day. (A boat is said to be on the collar when it's safely moored near shore. (Collar refers to the means used to moor the boat, which is usually a killick with one end of a rope or chain fastened to it. This is thrown into the water about 30 yards from shore. The other end of the chain or rope stays afloat by means of a large stick or buoy).

~ Chapter Eighteen ~

You Hum It And I'll Play It

While most people on Indian Islands could have a drink in their homes, many did not and whether this was for family or religious reasons, I'm not sure. Those people would, however, sneak a drop out in the store. Everybody had a store where food such as pickled cabbage in beef barrels and salted salmon in boxes was kept, as well as dried codfish, flour and other staples.

Because there was no refrigeration, the only way to preserve cabbage was to keep it in pickle in an empty barrel. Suitable amounts of salt and water were mixed to make a pickle and the cabbage was put in until the barrel was filled and the cabbage covered in brine.

There's a great story told about a party which took place in one of these stores about a week before Christmas. It is alleged that a chap known as Uncle John had a brew of beer out in his store. The beer was kept warm by the pot bellied stove which he had installed there. He was one of those fellows who was not allowed to drink in his house. As a warm-up for Christmas he invited a few of his buddies to the moonshine running off process. They started running off the moonshine, having a scattered drink as it became available.

Now Uncle John was a good accordion player and he made sure he kept that in the store. After a few drinks they got in a rollicking mood, and Uncle John started playing the accordion. Everyone joined in the dancing, which continued for the playing of several jigs and reels. Finally, Uncle John, wanting an excuse to have a break so that he could get a drink, said his fingers were tired and he would have to stop for a while.

They all re-filled their glasses and looked around for a place to sit down. Uncle John half sat on the top of a barrel of pickled cabbage. There was no cover on the barrel. One of the guests said, "Uncle John, do you know your ass is in the pickle?"

"No, my son," he said, " but if you'll hum it, I'll play it."

~ Chapter Nineteen ~

The Fishery of 1938

The chief fishery when I was growing up was the cod fishery. The fish was salted, washed and sun dried for the Spanish, Portuguese, Italian and West Indian markets. This product was exported from all the major ports in the province. Our fish was moved through Fogo.

Other species of fish were available but no market had been developed for them at that time. Caplin, for instance, was of no economic value. A few were cured for local consumption but the main use was fertilizer for the gardens. Lobsters were very plentiful but there was no fresh market. Lemuel Hoddinott and George Day of Perry`s Island operated lobster canning factories as a sideline operation. Salmon were plentiful. Some were consumed locally and some were salted mainly for the Lenten season. Squid and herring were harvested for bait only.

Fishing patterns were not too different from those experienced today. Some years the fish did not appear inshore. There were years when schooners returned empty from Labrador. It was a phenomenon which was attributed to inadequate snow fall, low run off of fresh water affecting the temperature of the salt water.

The failure of the inshore fishery, and there were many, was not blamed on excessive offshore fishing, because there was no offshore fishing effort. Landings were up and down, prices also fluctuated. We were never able to match up high landings with high prices. There were no support programs such as unemployment insurance so many fishermen and fish merchants experienced some very lean years.

The last year I fished was in 1938. when my brother, Harvey, and I undertook a joint operation. My father made major repairs to our boat during the winter, and Harvey and I made a large new cod trap. It would float in 18 fathoms of water, was 120 yards on the round, and equipped with 80 fathoms of leader. We used a ship's anchor which we purchased from Pat Newman of Boyd`s Cove to moor the trap. We also had two smaller cod traps. When spring arrived we engaged four sharemen, two each. They were Stanley Kinden, Uncle Allan Sheppard, Jimmy Collins and George Gale.

During the caplin scull we used the two small traps in berths around the islands. Later we set our big trap at Cape Fogo. The cod trapping season was generally from June 15 to August 15 with July being the most productive period. We had a successful summer, landed 700 quintals of fish. In the fall, we fished hook and line at Little Fogo Islands. When all of our fish had been dried and shipped, we proceeded to Fogo to settle our accounts for the year. When all the bills were paid I was $12 in debt. I resolved then and there that fishing was not for me.

My father and mother often implored me to go get some learning in my head and get away from the fishing boat. That was the advice most parents were offering their children at that time. I was already a proficient wireless operator and knew the post office business. The next year I found my first job with the Department of Posts & Telegraphs.

~ Chapter Twenty ~

My First Job

"Get your education, my son and get away from the fishing boat," was a phrase which still lingers in my mind. My father and mother were determined I would get a better chance in life than them. It`s a terrible indictment of what was our main industry, but it reflected how most parents thought about it in the 1920`s.

I managed to graduate with Grade XI when I was 14 years of age. By that time I was also a competent wireless operator, proficient in the use of both the continental and International Morse Codes. The telegraph offices were operated by the Newfoundland Department of Posts and Telegraphs. In the progress of learning wireless telegraphy, I also learned the Post office operations. The two main reasons for my pursuing a career in that profession were (1) my father was a postmaster and two of my sisters, Lydia and Meta, were wireless operators (2) it was one of the better employment opportunity areas.

While much of my wireless telegraphy training was done at home, Miss Lulu Pennell of Carmanville, the wireless operator at Indian Islands, was my main instructor. Her practice of allowing me actually send and receive telegraph traffic to and from the other offices helped me immeasurably.

In 1939, when I graduated from high school, my sister Meta (Carol, as she prefers to be known) was postmistress and operator at Windsor, in central Newfoundland. The position of assistant in that office became vacant, and she wrote to my mother suggesting I should apply for it.

I wrote an application and to the surprise of all I was accepted for the job. The pay was to be $39.50 per month, not much money even by 1939 standards. However, it was a job and I was happy to accept it. I was required to assume duties at Windsor as soon as possible. My trip started in late May.

Due to lingering ice as a result of severe winter conditions travel off the island was difficult. It was necessary that I get to Lewisporte and then by train to Windsor. I had never been to Lewisporte and never seen a train. Luckily for me, my Uncle Allan Sheppard was about to leave for his summer employment, operating a logging camp at Deer Lake. Frank Saunders was going to St. John`s to take up his position as engineer on the schooner, Maxwell R. Corkum, which was engaged in the coastal trade. Gregory Gale was also ready to leave for St. John`s to assume his role as mate on the Bell Island ferry. They all agreed to let me go along with them. We contracted with Uncle Al Collins (no relation) to get us off the island to a point on the mainland where we could get to Lewisporte. He owned a regular trap skiff about 38 feet in length. There was plenty of ice around when his boat was launched and made ready. The next morning we boarded her with practically all of the residents of the island on hand to say good bye as we slipped the bow line and departed for Boyd`s Cove.

We made very slow progress due to heavy ice. Many times it looked as if we would have to turn back, but we eventually arrived at Blind Tickle. It was impossible to go further. The skipper decided we would disembark and walk overland and the boat returned to Indian Islands.

This was quite a trek in the spring of the year with the ground soft, muddy and wet and sometimes icy, with little more then a woods path to follow for 30-35 miles.

We took our luggage, I had one small suitcase, the men carried back packs. They helped me tie my suitcase to my back freeing up my hands and we began the trek through the woods towards a small community called Port Albert. We arrived there some time after dark and stayed overnight with a couple whose names were Day. The next morning we started early and arrived at Boyd`s Cove just before dark. We spent the night with a Mr. and Mrs Freake, who operated a boarding house.

Walking through the country was very difficult. Most of the snow and ice on the land had melted and the ground was soft and muddy. Mr. Freake owned a horse and during the night Uncle Allan persuaded him to haul our luggage to Lewisporte. We were to follow on foot. I don`t recall how much he charged for the trip but we left bright and early next morning. We covered the distance to Birchy Bay during the day and since it was a fine night we walked on to Campbellton. We stayed with Mr. Lewis Hill and his family. He had five or six beautiful daughters who later moved to Glenwood. In conversation with Mr. Hill, he told us that Lewisporte was still frozen over. The winter ice had not yet broken up. The temperature was a little below freezing and the men figured the ice would be stiffened enough for us to walk on. To take advantage of the freezing temperatures, we would need be on the ice early, before the warmth of the sun could melt the nights freezing.

We left Campbellton quite early, timing our arrival at Michael`s Harbour on the south side of Lewisporte at daybreak. We were reluctant to enter upon the ice before daylight. The plan was for Greg Gale, Frank Saunders and I to walk across the bay to the north side of Lewisporte where the railway station was located. This would eliminate 8 or 9 miles off the walk around the bottom of Lewisporte. Uncle Allan was to go the long way around in company with Mr. Freake and the horse hauling our luggage. At dawn, as the sun came up, we started our trek over the ice towards the pier and railway station, some three or four miles distant across the bay.

At the beginning of our walk the crust on the ice could withstand our weight. As we progressed our feet would sometimes break through and we could never be sure how safe the ice underneath might be. We walked at a brisk pace trying to beat the melting effect of the sun until Greg Gale complained of snow blindness. He was so seriously handicapped one of us had to lead him by his arm. At last we arrived close to shore only to come on a channel of open water about 30 ft. wide. A small ice reinforced boat had entered Lewisporte during the night and we could see her tied to the pier. We debated turning back but concluded the ice would be too soft for us to try that. The alternative was to find enough small pieces of ice to enable us to copy or tabby (copy and tabby both refer to the act of jumping from one floating ice pan

My Work Life

to another) across the channel. Some people on shore saw us and recognized our predicament. They came with ropes and long poles to assist us, by positioning the broken pans of ice left in the wake of the ship. We finally crossed the channel. Greg, being snow blind, fell in the water and got wet but he was none the worse for that by the time he joined the train at 6:00 p.m. bound for Notre Dame Junction to connect with the No.2 Express from Port aux Basque enroute to St. John`s. Frank Saunders left with him.

There was no westbound train until the following night so Uncle Allan decided he and I would walk to Salt Pond, now called Embree. It is a community about five miles down the bay from Lewisporte and two of his daughters, Alice and Doris, were married and living there.

There was a well worn path to Embree but walking had now become a burden for me. I developed pain (stitches) in my upper stomach in the diaphragm area and was obliged to take several spells. At each stop. Uncle Allan would put a small rock in my mouth under my tongue and bend my head forward between my knees. This was supposed to help alleviate the pain. You know what? I believe it helped!

At any rate, we finally arrived at Embree and remained overnight. The following afternoon, much refreshed, we returned to Lewisporte. We boarded the train at 9:00 p.m. and I had my first train ride. We went as far as Notre Dame Junction, where we joined No. 1 Express from St. John`s to Port aux Basques. I arrived at Windsor (Grand Falls station as it was called then) around 11:30 p.m. My sister, Meta, was there to meet me. We said our good-byes to Uncle Allan and I proceeded to my boarding house, which Meta had arranged for me.

The people with whom I boarded were Mr & Mrs Archie Peckford. He was the manager of the Singer Sewing Machine Company. They lived in an apartment located over the store on Main street opposite the railway platform. Next morning I proceeded to the office which was about two blocks down the street. It was a very busy office and I enjoyed it very much. I did most of the post office work until I became accustomed to the land-line telegraph sound. It was entirely different from the wireless or radio sound, which I was used to. I soon mastered it and from then on I helped out by sending and receiving some of the many telegrams which were handled in the office.

My Work Life

Johnny Cardoulis, who would later become the Fire Marshall for the United States Air Force base at Fort Pepperrell in St. John's and, still later, Fire Commissioner for Newfoundland and Labrador, was the assistant at Grand Falls. Johnny and I became good friends and went fishing quite often at Rushy Pond. We met again when I worked on our USAF contract during my days with CNT. I was a member of cabinet when Johnny was appointed Fire Commissioner.

Many times during the summer I became rather homesick, but Meta encouraged me to stay on. When war was declared in September 1939 I was really worried, and more than a little scared. The Nazis were over-running Europe and everyone was expecting the worst to happen.

It was a very worrisome period of my life.

~ Chapter Twenty-one ~

My First Office: Harbour Deep

In the spring of 1940, the position of postmaster/operator was advertised in the community of Harbour Deep. I applied for the position and was successful. I went back to Indian Islands for a couple of weeks before proceeding to Harbour Deep.

The way to get to Harbour Deep was by the coastal boat service. I could join the boat at Twillingate or St. John`s. While sitting around the supper table one evening. the family wondered whether I might be able to join the Ranger as she passed through Stag Harbour, about two miles from Indian Islands as that would eliminate a trip to Twillingate. I telegraphed Mr. A. J. Ivany, the secretary for posts and inquired if he could intercede on my behalf and arrange for the Ranger to stop and pick me up while going through Stag Harbour Run. The next day, I received a message confirming that Captain Jimmy Snow of the Ranger would pick me up at mid- afternoon on Friday. That afternoon, when we saw the Ranger approaching from the east Harvey and my father and I boarded the I`m Alone and left to intercept her. The Ranger didn't stop, she merely slowed down. We motored alongside, a ladder was lowered, and with my small suitcase in hand I scampered up the side and onto the deck. Practically all the passengers and crew witnessed the boarding. My heart sank a little when the I`m Alone veered away and left, but I was soon immersed in the crowd of passengers and made the best of it.

My Work Life

Our ports of call were Twillingate, Little Bay Islands, LaScie, Pacquet, Horse Islands, Coachman`s Cove, Baie Verte, Seal Cove, Wild Cove, Hampden, Sop`s Arm, Jackson`s Arm and then Harbour Deep. People were then living in Little Harbour Deep and Big Harbour Deep. Both places are located in the bottom of a beautiful fjord.

Elsie Murcell was the postmistress and operator, she belonged to Harbour Deep. She was being transferred to Seal Cove across the bay, and that created the vacancy which I would now fill. She was a beautiful girl and a good wireless operator. I was sad to see her leave. I boarded with her parents, Mr.and Mrs. Joseph Murcell. They ran a branch business for John Reeves Limited of Englee. The hills surrounding Harbour Deep are among the highest to be found anywhere in Newfoundland. This was quite a contrast to Indian Islands. The radio equipment in use was low powered, battery operated. To get a good signal in and out of Harbour Deep, the office was located near the top of the hills, I used to have to take a couple of spells on the way up. It provided a marvelous view of the community and the fjord. The community was split in two by the projection of a large cliff. To get from one area to the other a wooden walkway was suspended over the water, around the face of the cliff, for a distance of about two gunshots (a hundred yards). This was a very romantic setting and a favourite meeting place for young men and women. I still carry many happy memories of the summer I spent at Harbour Deep. The Murcells were great people and they looked after me very well.

Englee was the repeating office for all of White Bay. Roland Fox was the wireless operator there, and he was a good one. He was very impressed with my competence as an operator and was anxious to get me to move to Englee because the traffic was quite heavy there. In September Englee was declared one of several A.D.C. offices, and I was transferred there. A.D.C. meant Air Detection Centre. As a consequence of enemy submarine activity and vulnerability of our coastal shipping and communications, the RCAF established several listening ports around the island. Englee was one and I worked the night shift there, midnight to 9 a.m. Local shipping would report any unusual sightings or happenings at sea, and I would flash these reports to A.D.C. at Gander. We were also equipped to monitor wireless signals emanating from enemy shipping. All such information, of course, was coded.

My Work Life

I spent September, October and November and part of December at Englee, and thoroughly enjoyed my stay there. Bernard McDonald was the general manager of John Reeves Limited. I got to know one of his daughters, Bessie real well. His son Joe was also a good friend of mine. Roland Fox taught me a great deal about wireless telegraphy, and our paths would cross again in later years in Gander.

In order to handle the enormous amount of telegraph traffic, the island and Labrador were divided into sections. Each section had a collector or repeating office. The collector for the south coast was Placentia; for the northeast coast, Botwood, and for Conception, Trinity and Bonavista Bays it was Topsail. The northwest coast was taken care of by Bonne Bay. The places along the railway on the west coast were channeled through Port aux Basques and Corner Brook. St. John`s, of course, was the hub for all of the island and Labrador and where the head office was located. I was driven by ambition to reach headquarters. The natural progression was through the large repeating offices. In December, there was an advertisement that the department would receive applications from qualified personnel for a position of wireless operator at Topsail. Roland was very satisfied with my work, but he encouraged me to apply for the Topsail job because it would be a great promotion for me. I followed his advice and submitted an application. It wasn't long before I received a message saying I had got the job. The salary was $129.50 per month, the highest salary paid outside headquarters. I was tickled pink and felt I had the world by the tail. Arrangements were made for a replacement for me at Englee and I joined the Kyle on her last trip for the season to St. John's.

It was the practice in these days for businessmen from around the coast to go to St. John`s on the last trip of the coastal boat serving their area. For all practical purposes, the fishing season was over and all the fish had been shipped. Supplies had been received and stored for the winter. This trip was necessary to settle up accounts with the St. John`s traders and do Christmas shopping. In the event that sea navigation was closed by the time these businessmen were ready to return they would fly home. On this trip, the Pomeroys and Eliol Strangemore from St. Anthony were onboard. A Mr. Newhook from Roddicton and Bernard McDonald boarded at Englee. McDonald's son, Joe, who was home on leave from the

My Work Life

Navy, was also onboard, returning to duty. Joe and I were good buddies, even though we had only know each other for about three weeks.

The Kyle would berth at the government wharf at most of the ports around the bay. Seeing it was the last trip out of Corner Brook, the western terminus, she carried much freight. Sometimes we would be in port as long as three or four hours unloading supplies, and Joe and I would visit people he knew through his father`s business outlets around White Bay. The boat kept going, day and night, but there were some exceptions. On arriving at Jackson`s Arm, mid-afternoon, it was announced we would be staying there all night. We were notified that the enterprising ladies of the Anglican Church were having a rabbit supper in the parish hall. Captain Jimmy Wheeler left no doubt that he expected members of the crew and all passengers to attend. In this way we would be providing much needed financial support for the community effort.

The funniest thing happened that night. Joe McDonald, his father, and I went along with the captain and officers and other businessmen for the first serving. We entered the hall, were seated, and everything was going fine. Busy women dressed in clean white aprons were serving. The rabbit soup, more like stew, was delicious and the conversation was stimulating. When we were about midway through our tea and dessert Eliol Strangemore stood up. When he got the attention of everyone present, he begged to be excused and said he had to leave to get his skin. The language was such the people were shocked, you could have heard a pin drop.. Silence was replaced by giggling by some women. As visitors, we felt very embarrassed and the captain apologized as we thanked our hosts and quickly left for the ship. We were all ready to murder Strangemore when he finally returned . But we were quickly disarmed when he produced a fox skin informing us that was the skin he wanted to get. We later found out he was buyer and seller of furs, which he referred as skin.

By the time we arrived at Jackson`s Arm, the passenger liquor supply was becoming exhausted. Joe was in the navy and was used to taking a drink now and I passed for someone older so it wasn't unusual for me to be offered a drink as well, With supplies almost exhausted, Joe and I used to go ashore and search for moonshine. It was a known fact that the local people had a reputation of making good shine. Now, the people were most cautious and unless they knew you your chances were slim. Joe was looking forward to reaching Coachman's Cove. He knew some people there who surely would have a supply and he was confident they would sell us some. We arrived at Coachman's Cove early in the morning, Joe and I were up dressed and ready.

The Kyle docked at the Norris Premises, the biggest business in Coachman's Cove. Unfortunately, most of the people lived on the other side of the cove about a half mile away, accessible only by boat. A fifteen foot boat, equipped with two pairs of oars, and belonging to the Norris firm was tied to the wharf. We asked the people on the wharf if we could use it to cross the cove. No one took the responsibility of lending it to us so we decided to assume the responsibility ourselves and took the boat. We were told we would be in port about two more hours, which we thought would give us ample time to row across the cove and back.

The wind was with us and the water was shallow on the other side where docked. There was a long walkway from the shore to the stages and, from where we docked, a very long stagehead as well. We made fast the boat and walked up to the narrow road which served the community. Many people were still in bed. Those who were up had lit fires and we could see the smoke rising from their chimneys. It was cold and there was at least three or four inches of snow on the ground.

The first house we went to, Joe knocked on the door and made his pitch for moonshine. We had no luck but we continued on, visiting five or six houses and still no luck. Some people professed complete ignorance and others said they had some moonshine but it was all gone, and so the excuses went. We decided to keep trying, and at this one particular house an elderly lady answered the door. Joe made his usual plea, but all we got in return was pity and concern for our warmth. We weren't dressed for the cold temperature. As we were about to leave she asked who we were. Collins meant nothing to her, but the name McDonald caught her attention. "Where are you from?" she asked. Joe said he was from Englee and added that his father's name was Bernard. That did the trick. "Glory be to God," she said, "come in."

She knew Joe's father quite well from some years before. While she was asking all sorts of questions, she fetched a bottle of moonshine and two glasses. I had a couple of drinks, but Joe had more and they were large. I knew by this time the Kyle would soon be ready to leave and I tried to get Joe to return to our boat. It took some persuading, but I finally convinced him to leave. That adorable lady gave us two bottles of moonshine. It was in Main Brace Rum bottles. Just as we arrived at our boat the Kyle sounded her whistle, which meant she was departing the pier. I looked over and sure enough she was beginning to move. I was concerned but Joe didn't seem to attach much urgency to our situation. As the sun rose the wind increased and was now against us and blowing quite hard. Although Joe was in the navy he was awkward with the oars. He was more hindrance then help so I persuaded him to let me do the rowing.

The Kyle was now heading out the cove at a fairly fast clip and I realized we had to intercept her. I could see myself caught in Coachman's Cove all winter and that was not part of my plan. The fear of that happening, coupled with the fact that I was mad at Joe, gave me extra strength to row hard. I believe I was going as fast as the Kyle. At any rate, I intercepted her and threw a rope to a crew member on the quarter rail. We damn near upset the boat because when the rope came taut we were pulled under the quarter of the large ship Kyle which soon slowed down and we were pulled up along at midships. We attracted a lot of attention right from the bridge down and including the passengers. A rope ladder was dropped over the rail and I secured the end of it. Joe by now was in very poor condition and such that he couldn't make it up the ladder. With the help of a member of the crew above and me below, we got him over the rail and onto the deck. I soon reached the deck with my bottle and what was left of Joe's. He had been sampling his crossing the cove.

By this time we were well out of Coachman's Cove and the bosun asked me what will we do about Norris's boat. I said I suppose d we would have to take her onboard. He said that wasn't possible and there was only one alternative, and that is to cut her loose. He dropped the rope in the head of her and we steamed away. I presume someone in Coachman's Cove retrieved the boat. At any rate, we heard nothing about the matter and I was reluctant to make inquiries. In the eyes of the passengers we were both heroes, but the captain thought we were pretty careless. Everything was forgotten, however, after we shared our moonshine.

The weather was quite cold and ice was forming, especially in the bays. When we arrived in Twillingate we were informed that the Kyle was being diverted to Botwood. A paper carrier was caught at Botwood and the Kyle was needed to break a channel through the ice. The Kyle was a good ice breaker, and the following morning we left Twillingate and proceeded up the run towards Botwood. An ore carrier enroute to Botwood for a load of ore concentrate from Buchans followed us up the bay. We arrived at Botwood in late afternoon, bringing the ore boat in, and leaving a channel for the paper carrier to reach the open sea.

We joined the train at Grand Falls and I proceeded to St. John's on my way to take up my position at Topsail.

~ Chapter Twenty-two ~

The Unsettled Years: Topsail Experience

I arrived at Topsail and started work around the middle of December. I was boarding at Geehan's Hotel A fellow by the name of Ern Chislett was the officer in charge. Things were pretty hectic as message volume was high and we were required to work every night from 7 p.m. to midnight, in addition to our day shift of 9 a.m. to 1 p.m. and 2 p.m. to 6 p.m. This was known as the pre-Christmas rush. There was no telephone service around the coast of Newfoundland, people could not talk to relatives and friends as they do today and the only means of communication, other than mail, was the telegraph message.

To ensure Christmas greetings were received in time, people began sending them around the middle of December. These messages took second place to all other messages and were sometimes delayed as the system could handle only so much traffic. The department supplied suggested texts for the messages and they were written on a special Christmas decorated form. In the process of transmitting, the messages were identified by the sending operator "CTG" meaning "greeting." When this signal was flashed, the receiving operator put a greeting form receiving sheet in his typewriter. The message was delivered to the addressee in a suitably decorated envelope.

Sending operators identified other traffic as "ORD" meaning "ordinary full rate message." Urgent messages were

My Work Life

identified as "pink" and were written and received on pink paper, as opposed to white paper for ordinary messages. Messages of greeting had a low rate if suggested texts were used. A higher rate was charged for ordinary messages and still higher rate was charged for a pink message. The lines were always jammed with ordinary and pink messages. One can imagine then how things became really clogged when Christmas greetings were added.

During the year we were paid at the end of the month. Due to the need for additional money at Christmas time, and as a gesture of goodwill in lieu of overtime, our December cheques arrived just prior to Christmas. The cheques were dated December 31, but I never had any trouble cashing it. When I received my cheque at Topsail, it was in the amount of $89.50 not the $129.50 I had been told I would be paid. The man in charge of the Department of Posts and Telegraphs was Mr. A. J. Ivany. His title was Secretary of the Department. All departments heads were called secretary, instead of deputy minister, as we know them today. Anyway, I was paying $60 a month board so it was important for me to get my finances in order. I sent a telegram to Mr. Ivany requesting the balance of my pay. I was shattered when I received the following reply from him:

"REGRET, DUE TO TREASURY BOARD REGULATIONS WE ARE UNABLE TO PAY THE ADVERTISED RATE FOR THE TOPSAIL POSITION STOP TO QUALIFY FOR THE HIGHER RATE YOU MUST BE EIGHTEEN YEARS OF AGE OR OVER." (Signed: A. J. Ivany)

What this meant was that I would still be paid my Englee rate of $89.50 even though I was doing the same amount of work as the other guys at Topsail. I felt betrayed. Why didn't someone advise me of this requirement before I was appointed? My records told them I was only 15 years of age. We had a telephone to St. John's and I placed a call to Mr. Ivany, but he refused to talk to me about the matter. I knew I wouldn't be able to afford to pay $60 a month for board and find money for the other basic purposes on $89. 50. I was also expected to send money home to my parents. How would I explain it to them? I had always been able to send them money on my previous salary. I explained the situation to Ern Chislett, the officer in charge, there was nothing he could do. I decided to go to St. John's and see Mr. Ivany. Ern thought this would be an exercise in futility and, furthermore, he couldn't do without me because messages were really piling up. Whatever the consequences, I took the next morning's bus to St. John`s. When I walked into the headquarters offices everyone expressed great surprise and shock. Derry (D. R. Clarke), who later became district director for Canada Posts in Newfoundland, was the staff clerk. He told me I should be in Topsail working like everyone else. He also informed me that Mr. Ivany was terribly disturbed over the action I had taken and still refused to see me.

I said, "Derry, you better tell him. If he wants me to go back to Topsail he had better let me discuss things with him."

Derry was as white as a sheet but to his credit he delivered my message. When he returned, he said Mr. Ivany would see me in a few moments. In a few minutes, Derry led me to Mr. Ivany`s office and left as soon as I stepped inside. Mr. Ivany was seated behind a huge desk when I confronted him. I explained the situation to him and he said, " You have a duty to be back in Topsail doing your work, and I won`t tolerate your insubordination. You upstart young fellows expect and demand too much. A boy of your age should be more than pleased with the amount we are paying you." He said he didn't write the Treasury Board regulations, but it sure sounded as if he was the author.

I said, " Mr. Ivany, it`s not my fault that I`m only 15 years old. I was appointed to a job which supposedly would pay me $129.50 per month. I`m doing my work and doing it well. Had I known I would not be paid for it I wouldn't have moved to Topsail."

We had reached an impasse. He hid behind his desk and the Treasury Board regulations. I stood on the principle that a trust was broken and from a financial point of view I could not return to the Topsail office. As reluctant as I was, I had no alternative but to resign. I requested the appropriate form and did so. He was furious. He said, "You`ve left us shorthanded at Topsail at the worst time of the year." I responded by saying, "Yes, and you have left me without a job at a critical time in my life."

I returned to Topsail, picked up my clothes, paid my bill at Geehans, said good-bye to Ern Chislett and the other operators and left for an uncertain future in St. John`s. My sister, Meta, was now working there and boarding at Mrs. Abbott`s on

Brazil Square. I arranged a room there and started a search for another job. I had no qualifications for anything other than wireless telegraphy. I went to Western Union and Canadian Marconi, but they had no vacancies. Finally, I found a job as a warden at the Hospital for Mental & Nervous Diseases on Waterford Bridge Road. It was on the maximum security floor. I got a boarding house in the general area and started work. I worked a few shifts and soon realized I wasn't cut out for that type of work and I left.

My parents were now aware of my predicament and they had been in touch by letter with my stepbrother, Albert, and stepsister Muriel, who were living in Sydney, Nova Scotia.. They got in touch with me and invited me to Sydney where there would be no trouble to find employment. The alternative was to go back to Indian Islands. I decided to go to Sydney, and around the end of January I departed by train for Port aux Basques and the Gulf ferry to North Sydney.

The train trip across the island was quite uneventful, but the Gulf crossing was a different matter. We were caught in a vicious storm. The boat became iced up to a dangerous level. I believe I was the only person onboard who was not seasick. At a time much later than scheduled we docked at North Sydney. Albert and Muriel were there to meet me. After clearing Canada Customs and Immigration, we departed for Muriel`s home at 39 Victoria Road in Sydney. I was in a foreign country. Muriel`s husband, Aubrey Hines, worked in the steel mill, while Muriel operated a small bakery and confectionary store. I helped her out until I found a job with a salvage company, down by the railway station, owned and operated by a Scotsman by the name of Sandy Ferguson.

Albert had more room than Muriel because he had a smaller family so I moved in with him and his wife, Aubrey, and their three children. The job at Fergusons gave me a pay cheque until I could find something better. After a month or so I found a job with Canadian Comstock Company, an electrical construction and consulting firm. My work took me to the naval base at Point Edward , and consisted mainly of repairing electrical and electronics equipment on allied and Canadian warships damaged in the Battle of the Atlantic. It was a much more rewarding job, and I was happy. The company personnel and co-workers were very fine people, however, I still missed the Continental and Morse codes. I missed no opportunity in getting to know the wireless setup onboard the ships and became acquainted with several operators who were naval personnel. Unknown to my parents, I tried to enlist, but was too young. I worked all winter and when spring came I received a letter from Meta, who was still in St. John`s. She told me she had been speaking with Mr. Ivany and Derry Clark. They had both asked how I was doing and said if I wanted to come back they would find something for me.

I decided to give Canada a try, but as time wore on I became affected with the age old Newfoundland urge to return to the island and the romance of Morse Code was also a strong draw. I decided to write to the Department of Posts & Telegraphs to inquire if any positions were available. In no time at all I received a reply offering me the position of postmaster and operator at Gander Bay. If I was interested, I was to take up duty there as soon as possible.

At first, it seemed like a step backwards, considering the class of office. However it was near home at Indian Islands, and it allowed me to once again resume the type of work for which I was trained and liked. I accepted the job over the objections of my relatives and friends at Sydney. I arrived in Gander Bay in May 1942, just a few days after my seventeenth birthday. It was a custom in Newfoundland outports for someone to meet the school teacher and/or the wireless operator when they arrived in the community. In Gander Bay, when the Glencoe arrived in the afternoon, I was met by Mrs. Katie Peckford, her daughter Joan, and Mrs. Annie Ford. Katie would later become my mother- in- law and Joan my wife.

Upon completion of the usual greetings I left to go up the shore with Mrs. Ford, who was to be my boarding mistress for my first year at Gander Bay. When we got to Mrs. Ford's house I met her family, had a quick lunch, then proceeded to the office and met Mrs. Winnie Saunders who was filling in until I arrived.

Joan`s dad was Joe Peckford, the local manager of the Horwood Lumber Company. Her mother, Kate, was a former wireless operator who had met Joe when she was sent to Gander Bay. Kate handled all of the incoming and outgoing mail and telegrams for the company and consequently was a frequent visitor to my office. On most occasions she brought Joan with her. Joan was then 14 years old and very soon she was given the responsibility to handle her father's mail. This meant she was required to visit the office at least twice a week. She was still attending school and on many afternoons after school she would turn up at my office. We soon developed a very close relationship and it was not unusual for me to be invited to her house for Sunday dinner. Her father and mother always treated me kindly and he and I got along extremely well. Her parents were both strong anti-confederates and strong Tories. I had some strong political views myself, but in all honesty I was more interested in Joan than politics. When she relieved her mother as organist at the church on Sunday evening service my attendance really improved. I would always take her home after church ,though by circuitous routes.

Indian Islands was about 20 miles out the bay and I was anxious to visit my parents who at this time were living there alone. Max Gillingham, a close friend, loaned me his boat for the trip. He owned a river boat equipped with a 20 HP Evinrude outboard motor. Joan decided to make the trip with me and we left on Saturday morning with the idea of returning on Sunday evening. Those river boats are not constructed to handle big waves but the weather was good and we encountered no difficulty. I asked my parents if they would like to come to Gander Bay for the winter if I could find suitable living accommodations..They thought it was a great idea and when I returned I found a house which we rented and they joined me in October. They moved back to Indian Islands the following May, and they did this again the next year. Joan was a big hit with them and their love for her was only surpassed by mine.

~ Chapter Twenty-three ~

The Wreck of the Acme

In 1943, I was employed with the Department of Posts and Telegraphs in Gander Bay and because of my junior status I didn't get my annual vacation until early October. My mother and father were still living on Indian Islands and I decided to spend my vacation with them and also help with the harvesting of the gardens and anything else that needed attention. The late summer and fall can have stormy periods with Newfoundland on the track of tropical storms and hurricanes which sometimes leave great destruction in their paths.

One of the worst storms experienced, hit the area that year. The wind was southeastern and while it didn't do a great deal of damage to our area it kept most people awake most of the night as Indian Islands was not much above the high water mark.. The next day, people were getting together in houses and stores and of course the topic was the storm and the fierceness of the wind. I remember that we were looking through the front window in our house when suddenly the top of the masts and sails of a schooner appeared over Perry`s Island marshes. Schooners could sometimes be identified by the shape and colour of its sails and my father quickly identified her as the Acme.

The Acme was a 100 ton, two master schooner. She was a former banking schooner, and legend had it she was involved in the rum running trade during the prohibition period in the U.S.

She was purchased by Skipper Al Collins in 1928 and used in the Labrador cod fishery. In 1938, he sold the vessel to Baird and Company of St. John`s, who owned a herring plant in Labrador. They hired Skipper Abe Penney, a former crew mate, as captain. The Acme was used in the coastal trade for much of the year, and then brought the fish plant's output of dressed herring and meal to St. John`s.

When we saw the Acme she was returning from Labrador with a load of fish products, mostly barreled herring and herring meal. George Hynes, my father and I went down on the shore and observed from the open door on the lee side of the store. The Acme was now in full view and what a sight. I can't think of anything more majestic than a fully loaded schooner under full sail in a strong wind. As we watched she turned to starboard and headed for the Tickle. What a sight she presented when she turned around Blundon's Island and approached the Tickle. As she entered the Tickle all her sails were lowered but the force of the wind in her masts and rigging drove her on. White foam was breaking from her bow and even though the anchors were dropped it did not impede her progress. It was now clear to everyone that she would soon be in the shallow waters of the west end of the Tickle. She ran upon the muddy sandy bottom near Phillip`s Island just beyond where Jim Hoddinott lived. With any wreck there was great concern for the crews safety but it was quickly established that all were safe.

The owners, Baird and Company, were notified and Sam Holmes of Seldom, the official wreck commissioner for the area, was instructed to proceed to the site and assume control of the vessel and her cargo. He declared the Acme a total loss and proceeded to make arrangements to salvage the cargo. He hired a couple of crews to do the work. My brother Harvey was one of them and he and Cyril Sheppard and I used our boat, the I`m Alone, and began unloading the cargo. It was easy work actually because the diesel operated deck donkey was still working and used to lift the barrels of herring out of the hole to the deck and then off the deck into our boat.

With a constructed contraption of ropes which was called a "par-buckle" we pulled the barrels from the boat to the wharf decking and then rolled the barrels over the wharf and onto the bank adjacent to our fish store. When all the barrels had been removed from the Acme, we proceeded to lift the bags of herring meal from the ship. This was stored in our stage and fish store. Some of the barrels were damaged and some of the bags of meal were wet but we salvaged most of the cargo.

Under the provisions of the salvage laws we were entitled to one third of the value of the salvaged goods. Baird and Company wanted the herring and meal and arrangements were made to have the goods picked up and delivered to St. John`s. It was early in the new year when a cheque for the sum of $1,900 was received to be shared equally among the 10 people who were engaged in the salvage operation. Four men took the cheque to the Bank of Nova Scotia at Fogo and the cash was distributed to the people involved. Harvey told me later that his share was worth more than his summer fishery. Eric Collins and Skipper Al Collins, a past owner, who were at Botwood when the Acme was lost, dismantled the wrecked schooner so bringing to an end the schooner's distinguished career.

~ Chapter Twenty-four ~

Gander Bay: My Other Home

My roots were deep and strong in Gander Bay. I had done enough moving around for someone much older than I was and I became concerned that my driving ambition might be misconstrued, itchy feet syndrome being something less than a desirable trait, so I settled down for a while.

I boarded for a couple of years then rented a house and my father and mother came and spent two winters with me. It was most convenient for me and, since they were getting up in years, it permitted us to have some time together. Remember, I left home at the very tender age of fourteen. My parents fitted in well at Gander Bay and developed some very close and dear friendships, as I did. However, before too long I once again began to get restless and wanted more of a challenge in my life.

The Department thought I was wasting my time at Gander Bay and should be utilizing my skills elsewhere. They wanted me to relieve in the larger offices, such as Botwood and Topsail. I also performed some inspection and training services for them. When May month arrived my father and mother would return to Indian Islands, to come back to Gander Bay in October. I would generally spend the summer doing relief work at Botwood and St. John's. I spent a part of the winter of 1945 at Fogo. Tom Loder, a Fogo boy who had previously worked as an assistant, returned from naval war

My Work Life

service. I was sent to train him for the position of postmaster and operator. Tom was very bright and soon learned all he needed to assume his responsibility. I did some inspections and, in 1947, went to La Scie to find a local person to train for the office in that community. I spent the summer there and trained a young lady by the name of Josephine Clance. She took over the office when I left. She was a very bright young girl and finished a training course, which normally took a year, in less than six months.

On my return to Gander Bay, I stayed over at Exploits, where Joan was teaching school, for a weekend. After that, I proceeded to Gander Bay for the winter, staying there until the spring when we entered Confederation with Canada.

I was at Gander Bay for most of the time between 1942 and 1949. In relative terms, Gander Bay was a thriving community. Two large sawmills were in full operation. Each of them kept one large schooner occupied, freighting lumber products to St. John`s and Conception Bay. From 50 to 60 men were employed in these mills from May until November. The rest of the year they worked cutting and hauling logs. Logs were also cut for the Horwood Lumber Company mill at Horwood.

A number of men were employed by Bowaters and the Anglo Newfoundland Development . Company at Bishop`s Falls, Badger and Robert`s Arm. They cut and hauled pulp wood to the river bank where it was floated and hauled to the mills. Much of the A.N.D. Company wood supply was floated down the Exploits river and its tributaries. Gander Bay men were great woodsmen and renowned river men who were in great demand for the annual spring drive on Noel Pond and Exploits River.

They were also famous for their boat building, witness the Gander River boats. As I recall it, anyone who was able to work found employment. Some of the older men spent the fall, winter and spring engaged in trapping. They too made a good living.

I was fascinated by the stories some of the people told about their trips in the country, as they called a trip in the woods. Some of those stories are told by Brett Saunders in his book "Rattles and Steadies." Because of my interest in these stories, I found myself spending a lot of time in the company of men like Brett Saunders, Uncle Joe Gillingham, Hezekiah Gillingham, Lewis Francis, Dick and Tom Gillingham, my father-in-law to be, Joe Peckford, and Esau Harbin. From time to time, I heard all of these men talk about endeavours which exposed them to great danger and caused much hardship.

Max Gillingham, Aubrey Saunders, Gilmore Hurley, Ray French, Lou Gillingham, Ivan Gillingham and many others of my age were very close friends and, with their girlfriends and wives, made up a very happy group. Joan`s brothers, Harvey and Reg, were also great company to be with. Harvey was married to Max Gillingham`s sister and Reg brought back an English girl, much to the dismay of many of the Gander Bay ladies. In spite of these friendships, though, I found myself gravitating towards some of the older people, enjoying the tales and their yarns. Uncle Joe, who lived near the office, was a great friend of everyone. His house was a nightly meeting place for telling stories and playing cards. I made sure that I spent at least one night a week there. Uncle Joe taught me how to catch trout and Max Gillingham taught me how to fly salmon. The trout were plentiful everywhere, even at Point Head, a place near the office. Gander River, of course, was rated among the better salmon rivers in Newfoundland.

One of my most outstanding memories is of a salmon fishing trip at First Pond Bar on the Gander River where a group of St. John`s businessmen had built a fishing cabin. Tom Gillingham had built the cabin for Frank O`Leary, Dr. Bliss Murphy, Gordon Higgins and another man whose name escapes me. It was called O`Leary`s Cabin.

In July of 1952, I received an important message for Gordon Higgins, a St. John`s lawyer and a member of the Confederation team, who was fishing at O`Leary`s cabin. The telegram required a reply and I was requested to hire a boat and take the message to him and get a reply. There weren't many idle boats around, so Max decided he would take me up after the office closed at 6 p.m. In the meantime, he fitted me out with rod, reel, line and some flies and indicated we would do some fishing. I had never fly fished before.

On our arrival at the cabin we were invited in for a drink and treated royally. I delivered the message to Higgins and obtained a reply, then we proceeded to an anchorage about 100 feet away on the bar where we began fishing, the guests at the cabin having already caught their limit of 10 for the day. While I found casting awkward at first I soon got the hang of it. The fish were coming over the bar in such numbers it

My Work Life

reminded me of caplin on the beaches at Indian Islands. I forget how many we boated but we sure hooked a lot of fish and, just before dark we left for the bay. It was a thrilling experience and I was to become hooked on salmon fishing, if you will excuse the pun.

I still can't figure out how after spending all these years in Gander Bay I had never salmon fished before. I suppose it was because I was absent most summers when the fish were running. At any rate, we made several trips that summer and one trip in particular stands out in my mind.

Max and I left in his boat and Aubrey Saunders came with us in his. It must have been Sunday because we all had the day off. We were headed for First Pond bar but the salmon were so plentiful on the lower part of the river that we never reached that far. Max and I fished from our boat and Aubrey fished from his. The boats were anchored in prime locations. Max had a straight leg which restricted his agility. After a few drinks he became rather clumsy. Furthermore, I was not yet accomplished at casting, so our lines became entangled a few times. I suggested to Max that he should put me out in a shallow spot where I could wade around and for him to take the boat by himself. He readily agreed to that. I walked down the river a little distance to a place called Jim Brown's Rattle. Gander Bay people called rapids "rattlers" and some of them called steadies "studies."

Max and Aubrey fished their way up to first rattle in their boats and I could see they were getting fish. I was not to be outdone and started to land some myself, but I lost a good many. The fish, right out of the salt water, were full of fight and I had not mastered the art of playing them. I don't think Max and Aubrey expected me to get many but it didn't take too long before I had four salmon landed and protected in a small pool which I had constructed near the shore. The sun was blazing hot and I realized my fish would nearly cook in the exposed area where I had them placed, so I constructed a shelter in a thicket of alders, covered them with wet palms and grass, and began fishing again. I landed one more fish and then Max and Aubrey arrived from up river. They had done quite well and asked how many I had caught. I said "Five." Only one fish was in sight and somehow I thought they didn't believe me when I said five.

They soon had a small fire going near the water's edge and boiled the kettle. They asked where my other four fish were. I was glad to show them, particularly as I had one fish which I guess would tip the scales at 9 or 10 pounds, with the others weighing in at about five pounds each. To my surprise, when I went to the spot where I had put my fish there were no fish there. Max and Aubrey had been moving around the area since they landed and I assumed they had played a trick on me. Meanwhile, they had come to the conclusion that I had caught only the one fish which I had with me when they arrived from up river. I tried to convince them I had four more fish, but no luck. After lunch, I started searching for my fish and my determination finally convinced them I must have more fish. They joined me in the search and very soon their hunting experience told them that an animal had been in the area, probably a fox. Before too long, Max found the salmon. The heads were eaten off two, including the big one, but two were intact. From the sign the animal left they were sure it was a fox. It must have smelled the fish and, even though it was only a few feet from me, dragged the four fish away to a spot 100 feet distant. It probably ate the two heads while we were eating lunch..This was to be my first experience with a fox, and it brought home the truth of Uncle Joe`s stories I used to hear about that wily animal.

~ Chapter Twenty-five ~

Uncle Joe's Horse

I may have mentioned before the very close friendship which developed between Uncle Joe Gillingham and me. He was severely handicapped in that one of his legs was bent and much shorter than the other. I don`t remember if it was the result of an injury or a birth defect but I suspect it was the latter. He kept active and did a lot of work, but he was unable to manoeuver through the thick woods. His wife`s name was Amy, Aunt Amy to everyone.

On one of my summer jaunts away from Gander Bay, my boarding mistress thought she would like to be relieved of the responsibility of boarding me. In a very friendly way she broke the news to me and said she had arranged for me to stay with Aunt Amy and Uncle Joe. They jumped at the chance to have me, and I thought it was a good arrangement too. I helped him out in many ways. Together we sawed and split the wood. On many occasions I brought the water in buckets from the well across the way. He kept a small pony named "Queen" and I helped him make the hay for feed and often fed the horse during the winter. He rewarded me by letting me harness Queen and go for a run on the sleigh. I found such outings most enjoyable.

Queen was equipped with a new harness and many bells. The driving sleigh was a piece of art. With an outfit like that, it was no trouble to attract a nice girl to go for a ride around the bay. Uncle Joe and Aunt Amy had two children, a son, Gerald, and a daughter, Ethel. They were both married. Gerald was working with Bowaters and living in Benton. Ethel was married to Matt Downer and lived at Main Point, about three or four miles down the bay from Clarke's Head, where we lived. Matt and Ethel visited us quite often and sometimes they would be accompanied by Matt's brother, Malcolm, who was much older than me, but single. Malcolm called me one day inviting me down to a party which he arranged for Saturday night. There was a hoot and holler phone system between the two places which we used to exchange telegrams. I wondered to myself if Uncle Joe would let me have his horse if I requested it. Over supper I mentioned the fact that I had been invited down to Malcolm's place at Main Point. He asked how I proposed to get there. The bay was frozen over quite firmly and even though the weather was cold I replied that I intended to walk. Without a thought, he offered the horse. He cautioned me about driving too fast. He didn't want her to sweat unduly. I was to put her in Matt's barn until I was ready to return. After supper I got ready. Uncle Joe helped me harness the horse and saw me off. In no time I was down to Main Point. We put the horse in Matt's barn and commenced the night's activities. Around two or three o'clock in the morning the party broke up and I made ready to return to Clark's Head. It was a beautiful moonlight night. With the snow on the ground and the ice on the water of the bay, I could see for miles. As I was about to leave, Malcolm warned me about a patch of very thin ice near the middle of the bay. He suggested I keep near the shore on the south side until I reached Harris Point. I could then cross the bay to Clarke's Head.

I set out with these instructions in mind. However, Queen had other ideas and insisted on taking the direct route home and there was no way could I keep her close to the shore. Suddenly Queen broke through the ice. To say I was frightened was an understatement. I tried in vain to get her out, but to no avail. The horse thrashed about for quite a while before becoming subdued. I was thoroughly soaked and making no progress towards freeing the horse .Fortunately for us both, Malcolm was watching my progress up the bay and saw what happened. He rushed to my assistance as fast as his legs could carry him. The strength of both of us was enough to get Queen back on the ice. We took the horse back to Main

My Work Life

Point and into Matt`s kitchen where we dried her off and kept her warm. The horse completely recovered and I left for home again around 9 a.m. I did not mention it to Uncle Joe because he might have been reluctant to let me have the horse again. Neither I nor the horse suffered any ill effects. From there on. I kept to dry land or well worn routes when traveling over the ice.

    The main reason for owning a horse was for hauling logs and fire wood from the forest in winter. There were several well traveled roads, such as Clarke`s Pond Road and Burnt Pond Road. These were used by many teams and the snow was well packed. Since the better trees near the main roads were already cut, men had to walk deeper in the forest to find suitable trees. In order to get the wood to the main road a path was cleared. Because these side roads were used less frequently the horse would very often get "stogged" in the snow. In such circumstances men would use pot lids or real snow shoes. Uncle Joe equipped his horse with four of these and it really helped the horse when the snow was deep.

Chapter Twenty-six

120's at Uncle Joe's

In the absence of theaters and television, one of the main pastimes in Gander Bay was playing cards. The most common game was called 120`s. From September until spring, cards were played almost every night in many homes and Uncle Joe`s was no exception. Since he was handicapped he preferred to stay at home so there was a card game in his house every night.

120`s was the only game played and the rules were agreed upon prior to the start of each night`s game. Different people played with different rules so it was necessary to establish the rules beforehand. Many of the people who played at Uncle Joe`s did not play in their own homes, the exception was Joe Peckford, my future father-in- law.

The regulars who played at Uncle Joe`s were Lewis Francis and Hezekiah Gillingham. Some nights Aunt Amy, who was a good card player, would join in with Uncle Joe and take these two on. Tom and Dick Gillingham and Joe Peckford were less frequent players, but if either of them arrived I would be conscripted to make up the sixsome. Sometimes they wouldn't need me and I was glad. I had other things to do, although I thoroughly enjoyed a game. I tried to keep my card playing to one night a week. Some nights more people would arrive than could be accommodated at cards as six was the maximum. Generally speaking, the first arrivals were given preference. The better card players generally arrived early to ensure themselves a seat.

Lewis Francis was always the first to arrive. It was said he ate at 4 o'clock to ensure his seat at Uncle Joe's card table. He would often arrive before Aunt Amy had time to get the dishes washed and taken off the table. He was a decent card player and he was always assured a seat. He had to pass by Hezekiah's house to get to Uncle Joe's and this was the signal for Hezekiah to also get on the move. He always apologized for coming in so early but everyone understood why he had to do it. He was a good player so this was not a problem. At my age there were other games that interested me more than playing cards. I was courting Joan at this time. Nevertheless I enjoyed a game once in a while. Most were very serious as winning was everything.

Tom was a terrible poor player, but he didn't give a damn. He seemed to get his kicks out of making mistakes and being ridiculed Dick, on the other hand, was very subdued and earnest, but he never really mastered the game. If he made a mistake he was seldom chastised. He seemed to attract more sympathy than wrath. Joe Peckford didn't play often enough to become expert but they respected him for this and enjoyed his company.

A typical game would find Uncle Joe seated at his end of the wooden table. The other would include Lewis, Henzekiah, Aunt Amy and one other, Tom or Dick or Joe, and myself. Uncle Joe would cast jacks to determine who would be partners. With that small detail decided, the sleeves were pulled up. As soon as Aunt Anne had the dishes cleaned and put away Uncle Joe would say "ok boys let's play cards.".At the start of the game things were rather tranquil. The same conditions applied if the bidders made their bid and conversely if the bidders were put down, but towards the end of the game when the teams were either winning or losing it was total bedlam. The old wood table took some pounding. Every time a player could beat the previous player's card he would hit the table with his bare knuckles. Some of those guys had big fists and knuckles like steel. I often saw the table boards split with these blows. Hezekiah was the hardest hitter and often injured his knuckles. I've also seen him take off his Smallwood- type boot and hit the table with it if he was playing the winning card at the end the game. Lewis Francis had a habit of keeping his pipe in his mouth, whether it was lit or not. Since most of his teeth were missing he held the pipe with one hand and if he had a big winning card to play he would leave the pipe to the security of his gums. Most times the pipe fell from his mouth with flankers flying over the table and in his lap, several times he caught his clothes on fire.

If a player made an error he was chastised and it was forgotten, occasionally though things degenerated into shouting matches. There were times when they didn't speak for days.

Passers by could always tell if cards were being played in a house. The houses were not insulated very well and the noise of fists hitting wooden tables could be heard some distance away.

Another great house for a good games of cards was Allan Harbin`s. Allan was a good player and his wife was an even better one. In the game of 120`s the ace of hearts was always a trump, rating next to the five and jack of the bid suit. It was said she came to the table with a supply of the ace of hearts up her sleeve. They all loved fun, food and drink and a good game of cards.

~ Chapter Twenty-seven ~

Snaring Rabbits

Most Newfoundland boys are familiar with snaring rabbits by the time they are nine or ten years old. Since there were no rabbits on Indian Islands, where I grew up I was denied that opportunity.

It was during my first winter in Gander Bay that I found out that everyone was doing it and I was left out. Rabbits were caught near the community and if you went farther, hundreds or thousands could be caught. These people supplemented their income by canning them and selling them commercially. Others took them to Glenwood and shipped them to St. John's to be sold.

Coupled with my ignorance of the art of snaring, I had another disadvantage. I was working six days a week and, Sunday morning by the time I fulfilled my religious responsibilities, I had little time left. If I lived in Gander Bay I knew I would have to prove that I could catch rabbits. With this in mind I resolved to find out all there was to know about this activity.

My boarding mistress Mrs. Ford's father, Maurice Hurley, who lived next door arranged to teach me everything I should know about snaring rabbits. In addition to the theory, I received practical, hands-on training and actually caught some rabbits just behind the Hurley property in company with Mr. Hurley. Soon I would strike out on my own.

During the fall and winter with daylight hours very short and working from 9 a.m. to 6 p.m. I didn't show my stuff till

My Work Life

the month of March. By then, it was late in the season and many of the rabbits had been caught. They become less discriminating about their trails and were more easily caught then, or so it is said. One day I got my snares ready, closed the office a little early, and walked in Clark's Road and ventured off into the woods not far from the community. There was still a sign of some rabbits around, so I put down about a dozen snares. I waited two days and nights before returning. When I checked the snares I had two rabbits, both still alive. I told Mr. Hurley and he said to make my snares a bit smaller.

My next trip I had two more live rabbits and I adjusted all my snares smaller. The rabbit season was to close on March 15 and that meant I had only a couple of days left before I would have to remove the snares. I planned to do this on the 15, which would be my last trip. When the day arrived a problem at the office delayed my trip to the woods. I had no choice but to retrieve them the following day. The next afternoon I left a bit early to ensure I would find them all. The first snare had a dead rabbit so the smaller size snare had worked. The next snare had a big brownish color cat in it. The cat was very much alive and quite vicious. Anyone who has snared a cat will know what I mean. I could 't get near it with my hands as I tried to free it. In a desperate attempt I used some snare wire to tie my axe to a long piece of wood. I took a swing at the snare and sure enough I cut the wire where it was holding the cat prisoner. The cat took off through the woods for home. I checked the remaining snares and removed them. I was just about to leave for home when I heard a man's voice nearby. This was Allan Peckford and he had a reputation as the crankiest old cuss in the bay. He quickly reminded me that the season was closed as he saw me take a rabbit from my snare and put it in my shoulder bag. He also informed me that the cat which I had snared belonged to him and he didn't like the manner in which I had released it and for that he was taking ne to court. By this time I was shaking in my shoes and the back of my neck was tingling. What a mess I was in! I figured the best defence was to say as little as possible. I returned home saying nothing about the incident to anyone, and to his credit he didn't either. I soon found out the cat wasn't his and it had survived the ordeal.

At least once every week I would drop over to Tom Gillingham's house for a drink of cold water. The drink was an

My Work Life

excuse to get the local gossip from Tom and Aunt Alice. I was invited in this day to the kitchen. No sooner was I seated on the wooden settle, when I noticed this brown cat lying underneath the wood stove. A comfortable place to lie down, warm and private. As soon as I recognized the cat he got up, stretched, eyed me suspiciously, and joined me on the settle. I was hoping the cat had a short memory of the treatment he got in my snare. To show my friendliness, I proceeded to rub the back of his head. Then Tom shouted, "My God, don't touch his neck, some son of a bitch caught him in a snare and the skin is torn in several places around his neck."

I quickly withdrew my hand, expressed pity for the cat, and said I hoped it would heal soon. I'm sure the cat recognized me because he kept staring at me all the while I was there. Eventually the cat's neck healed, and when it did I told Tom the story.

"You know," he said, "I had a suspicion it was your snare by the manner in which you responded to the cat's presence. At any rate, to catch a cat the snares were too big for a rabbit." His words confirmed what Maurice Hurley had told me.

~ Chapter Twenty-eight ~

Married to Joan

When Newfoundland entered into Confederation with Canada in 1949, the Department of Posts & Telegraphs responsibilities were split. The Canadian post office was given jurisdiction over the postal sector and Canadian National Telegraphs assumed responsibility for the telegraph side. Most employees were given a choice of remaining with the post office or going with CNT. I chose CNT and was offered the position of manager at Buchans where my salary would more than quadruple my salary at Gander Bay. I had a responsibility to send money to my parents but I knew with this new position I could also support a wife. I loved Joan very much and had no intention of going through life without her. Things were moving quickly and I was required to arrive in Buchans in 48 hours. On my last evening in Gander Bay I asked Joan to marry me. When she agreed, it was late at night and I was leaving the next morning. I thought we should consult her parents right away so we called them out of bed and they gladly agreed.

Next morning, Tom Gillingham took me to Glenwood in his river boat and I was off to Buchans while Joan and her mother started the wedding plans, assisted by my sister, Meta, in St. John's. Joan and I were married on September 19,1949, at St. Thomas`s Church in St. John`s by the Rev. Toope.

In 1950, CNT undertook a massive upgrading program. Telegraph and telephone services were upgraded and expanded and telex and radio services were introduced. To install, monitor and operate the necessary technical equipment, trained personnel were needed and so the Company invited applications from qualified employees to undergo technical training at the University of Western Ontario at London. I applied and, mainly because of my ICS training which I had done in Gander Bay, I was accepted. Seven of us from Newfoundlander joined 113 other students from all provinces and converged on London. The other members of the Newfoundland group were, Roland Fox, Reg Fallon, Bernard Prowse, Maurice Griffin, Doug Hookey and Fred LeBlanc. Upon completing our course of study we returned to Newfoundland. I accepted a position as early night repeater attendant at Corner Brook and Joan and our firstborn child, Brian, joined me there. We lived at first in an apartment at Pickering`s Inn then built a house in Corner Brook East, but didn't get to live in it for very long.

Career-wise, things moved rather quickly for me. After only a few months in Corner Brook, I was promoted to the position of manager. After a year in that position, I relocated to headquarters in St. John`s, where I became commercial inspector for the Newfoundland District, CNT. Joan and Brian, who had now been joined by daughter Betty, remained in Corner Brook until we sold our house. They then moved to St. John`s and we bought a house at 4 Rodney Street.

Although I had received much technical training I was now in the commercial field, with responsibility for all the island and Labrador, a job that involved much travel. I traveled the province several times, mainly by train and coastal boat.

~ Chapter Twenty-nine ~

My High Jump Record

In the fall of 1950, I was working with CNT and stationed in St. Anthony for about a month. I boarded with Uncle Johnny Newell and his wife who operated a large boarding house called the St. Anthony Inn. Just about everyone visiting St. Anthony stayed there. He and his wife were great cribbage players and they didn't often lose. I used to play with them when I could find a good partner. Our card games changed from cribbage to poker for two weeks in November. That came about because Capt. George Blackwood was staying with us. His schooner was badly damaged and was undergoing repairs at the dry dock in St. Anthony. Blackwood was an interesting character; while our poker stakes were small, he knew when to hold and when to fold.

His nephew, Eric Blackwood, who started Newfoundland Aviation which later became Eastern Provincial Airways, also stayed with us for a while. The storm which wrecked his uncle`s schooner also damaged his plane. It had been moored at the pier in St. Anthony and overturned, causing severe damage. In time, both the schooner and the plane were repaired and our friends went on their way. The weather was now turning cold and snow was expected anytime. One morning, when we were having breakfast, Mr. Newell said to me, "You are likely to see some dog teams today."

It had snowed overnight and he said no doubt some people would be harnessing up. Now I was always afraid of dogs, and I wasn't looking forward to seeing teams of them. Even one at

My Work Life

a time was too many for me. When I went outside to go to work, I figured there was about two inches of snow on the ground. I could tell that some teams had already been on the road. I could see the dogs tracks and the impression of the komatik. On the way to my office, in the government building, I had to pass by the Pomeroy property. The Pomeroys were business people and Roy Pomeroy lived in a big white house well back from the road. The front of the property was fenced with rails and palings. The palings were 6 feet high and about 4 inches wide. The space between each paling was the width of the paling. As I was approaching I saw a team of dogs coming up the road towards me. The dogs were quite frisky, barking and really traveling fast. A man at the rear of the komatik was shouting encouragement and instructions. I quickly decided I would be brave and remain on the side of the road until the team passed by, but that was not to be. It seemed as if the lead dog was headed straight for me. Fear struck through me. I ran towards Pomeroy`s fence and leaped over it. The fence was 6 feet high and I cleared it by what I thought was another 6 feet. I kept running towards Pomeroy house and there was one hell of a commotion behind me. The dogs were barking furiously, throats gurgling, and the owner yelling and cursing. I broke through Pomeroy`s door and straight through the house to the kitchen. My sudden entry startled them. It took some time before I could relax, and when I did we proceeded to the front of the house to see what had happened.

The team was made up of 10 dogs and they had gone through some openings in the fence and were hopelessly entangled. They were certainly chasing me and there was no doubt in my mind about what was their intention. The owner of the team was Mr. Penney from Pateyville and I think he cursed me more than the dogs. He said had I stood my ground nothing would have happened. I`m not convinced of that. Anyway, a 12 foot standing jump permitted me to escape and I want it put on record! Mr. Newell got a great charge out of it all, and so did my colleagues at the office.

~ Chapter Thirty ~

Postings to Corner Brook and then St. John's

When CNT posted me to Corner Brook I was assigned the early night shift, 4:30 pm until midnight, as wire chief. Joan and I had been married less then two years and had been living apart for much of that time. Consequently one of my first objectives in Corner Brook was to find a place where we could live. I was fortunate in locating a nice apartment in a six apartment building located across the street from where I worked and as quickly as possible Joan and our only child, Brian, joined me in the summer of 1951.

The apartment building was centrally located and that was a great convenience because I did not own an automobile. I was enjoying my work and Joan and I were enjoying living together in a nicely decorated and comfortable apartment.The building was heated by a hot water radiation system. The water was heated by an oil-fired furnace located in the basement. Our apartment had radiators in all the rooms and maintaining comfortable temperatures was accomplished by a thermostat which was located in the ground floor hallway. Around the end of October one of the tenants moved out and that ground floor apartment was let to an elderly couple. They were very friendly people but they sure didn't like too much heat and were constantly lowering the thermostat setting, resulting in lower temperatures in all the ground floor apartments, one of which was ours. Re-setting the thermostat became a cat and mouse game and in no time the landlord decided to relocate the thermostat to the elderly couple's

My Work Life

apartment thus making it inaccessible to the rest of us.

As the fall progressed and the outside temperatures continued to fall, our comfortable apartments living style continued to suffer. Day time temperatures while not comfortable could be tolerated but as soon as evening arrived sweaters for ourselves and blankets for Brian became the order of the day. We complained as did the other tenants but to no avail. I believe the two elderly tenants in whose apartment the thermostat was located must have had antifreeze in their blood. I also believe the landlord took advantage of the situation realizing there were savings in reduced heating costs. At any rate conditions continued to worsen and became more intolerable for us. The straw that broke the elephants back was one evening when I answered the telephone at work at around 9 p.m. Joan was on the other end and she was nearly crying and saying that unless some improvement could be made in the level of heat she would be forced to leave the apartment. Although I was quite busy I managed to run across the street to comfort her.

Every good wire chief carried long nose pliers, wire cutters and screwdrivers in his pocket. I made sure I carried mine. I entered our apartment and went to the hallway where I located the entrance to the basement of the building. Equipped with a flashlight ,which Joan had provided, I found the furnace and after some searching identified the thermostat wires. I quickly removed an inch of insulation from both wires, twisted them together, and the furnace immediately came alive. I didn't want to get caught doing this so I quickly left the basement and returned to the apartment. After reassuring Joan that the apartment would now warm pretty soon I left for the office. I had every intention to return to the basement and remove the short from the thermostat leads after the furnace was operating for an hour or so. Unfortunately, some emergency arose in Moncton, N.B. and I became really busy and totally forgot the furnace until my relief arrived and I left for home.

As I opened the door out of my office a very scary scene confronted me from across the street. All the windows and doors of the apartment building were open and the tenants were either standing in the doorways fanning themselves or they were standing outside. Immediately it occurred to me just what was happening and, if I needed to be reminded, the presence of an E..H Gullage plumbing and heating truck confirmed my suspicion. I entered the building and went straight to the basement. All of the Gullage technicians were there as well as the two landlords, whose names I shall not mention. Confusion ruled and nobody could determine why the furnace kept going or how to stop it. I suggested one way to stop the furnace was to cut of the fuel supply and everyone wondered why they hadn't thought of that. In an instant the valve was closed on the fuel line to the furnace and it stopped. Now the experts began to look for the real fault, but as this point the landlords decided that rather then pay overtime it was best to leave things for the night and return in the morning. Everyone left including me as things were getting back to normal upstairs. Without the furnace that night we realized things would be a bit cool, so extra blankets were spread on Brian and on our bed. Joan served up coffee and a light snack knowing that I planned to return to the basement as soon as it was safe. When all other people had retired I went to the basement location and removed the short from the thermostat wires.

In the morning as soon as the technicians arrived they restored the power and fuel and the furnace came alive again. I didn't stay around for fear my guilt might betray me.

During the fall the tenants on the ground floor threatened to leave unless the heating could be improved, and would you believe it, the landlord conceded and had thermostats installed in each apartment and we lived warmly for the remainder of our stay in that building.

I don't know if it is coincidence or not but one of the first pieces of legislation to be introduced and passed into law in the House of Assembly in 1972 when I became Minister of Municipal Affairs and Housing was The Landlord and Tenancies Act. That law was heralded as being long overdue and provided for major improvements in landlord and tenants relationships.

In the summer of my first year as manager of CNT in Corner Brook, I was honored with a visit by J.R.White, our General Manager out of Toronto and Mr. H. J. Clarke, our regional superintendent out of St. John`s. Since we were part of the Canadian National Railway system, they were provided a locomotive, a dining car and caboose for the cross island tour. After meeting all the staff and many of our preferred

My Work Life

customers, I was invited to dinner with them on board the dining car. After dinner and a lot of small talk, Mr. Clarke inquired if I would be interested in relocating to headquarters at St. John`s. I asked him what he had in mind and he said the company needed a commercial inspector and the position was mine if I was interested. I thanked them for the offer and told them I would let them know in a day or two.

When I went home that night I discussed the offer with Joan. After renting at three different locations we had just purchased a new home on Princess Avenue and we deferred our decision until the following day. Joan realized I was interested in getting ahead and she said if I wanted to accept the position then she was behind me. I called Mr. Clarke the next day and accepted his offer and it was agreed that I would assume the new position within two weeks. I left Joan with the responsibility of the three children we than had as well as the added burden of selling our house. Life was pretty hectic for a few weeks. I found and purchased a house at 4 Rodney St. in St. John`s at about the same time Joan had arranged the sale of our Corner Brook property and in no time we were settled away in our new home. My new work involved inspecting commercial offices throughout the island and Labrador, and it required extensive travel mainly by train and coastal boat. The commercial inspector's position was a new classification established in response to the tremendous need for training of our managers and agents and the necessity to carry out financial audits. The first two or three years I was extremely busy. A trip to Corner Brook, for instance, meant overnight travel to go and overnight to return. I tried to spend most weekends at home but found myself leaving the city on the 5 p.m. train on most Sundays, and was obliged to try and return to the city on Friday morning. This arrangement permitted me to spend Friday at the St. John`s headquarters to catch up on work there. Although so much travel was stressful from a family point of view, I have some fond memories of boarding train No. 1 at 5 p.m. on Sunday where I would have reserved a sleeping berth, which was a first class service. The sleeping cars were at the end of the train in front of the caboose and one or two dining cars were attached depending on the number of passengers traveling.

The first serving of dinner, which we called supper, took place prior to the train arriving at Holyrood. The dining cars

My Work Life

were equipped with very sturdy tables and chairs and an enclosed kitchen. White uniformed chefs prepared the food which was served by white uniformed stewards. I am not aware of any restriction on the employment of women on trains but I don't recall ever seeing a female cook or stewardess. The tables were immaculately decorated with the finest linen cloths and napkins and china and silverware which bore the Newfoundland or CN railway name. A superbly designed and professionally printed menu was supplied to each guest. A typical menu would offer a choice of soups or salads. An appetizer would normally be fried cod tongues or smoked salmon. The entree generally consisted of roast chicken, prime roast beef, various forms of lamb, pan fried codfish and baked salmon. Desserts were generally local berry pastries with ice cream and, while not included on the menu, after meal liqueurs were available at a reasonable price.

The table seated four people and created a great opportunity to meet strange and very often interesting people. To say the least, it was fine dining in a great setting and cordial atmosphere. After the meal I would go to the "smoker" for a cigarette.. The smoker was a small room which contained two stainless steel sinks, a private toilet space, one large chair and a bench which could accommodate four people. It was for the use of the sleeping car passengers. The porter would try and get a few winks of sleep on the bench after the passengers had all retired to their upper and lower sleeping berths.

My trips generally took me to Port aux Basques, Stephenville, Corner Brook, and Millertown Junction for connecting to the Buchans, Grand Falls, Gander and Clarenville.

I can say that my favorite porter was Jimmy Humphries. I could almost always depend on Jimmy to find me a berth wherever I might be joining his train, and besides that he was a great guy. I found train travel to be most relaxing and a rewarding experience even in winter, when the train was often delayed due to heavy snowfalls, particularly on the Gaff Topsails.

To visit costal communities, such as Twillingate, St. Anthony, Goose Bay and Bonne Bay, arrangements were made with the CN coastal boat service – the S.S. Glencoe serviced ports St. John`s to Lewisporte, S.S. Kyle serviced ports St. John`s to Nain and S.S. Northern Ranger serviced St. John`s to

Corner Brook. First class accommodations on the boats was referred to as staterooms. These rooms were generally above deck and were self contained, equipped with a bath and sink, a couple of chairs and a comfortable bunk. The dining room was equipped with eight to ten tables. The tables and chairs were chained to the floors, a necessary precaution for rough seas. Meal service was similar to that provided on the trains.

The most popular room on the boats was the smoking room. These rooms were equipped with a piano and quite frequently passengers brought along their own guitars and accordions. Late in the night the music and voices of the passengers could be heard around the ship.

~ Chapter Thirty-one ~

How's Your Mother?

When we joined Confederation in 1949, the standard of communications in the province left much to be desired, especially when compared with facilities on the Canadian mainland. Our system consisted mainly of direct current telegraphy, utilizing the Morse code as a means of transmission and a very inadequate telephone network. These systems utilizing outdated equipment were operated on open wire lines which were subject to many interruptions and at best provided poor quality transmissions. Canadian National Telegraphs immediately set out to improve this situation and undertook to construct a new pole line along the railway track from Port Aux Basque to St. John`s. The line was designed to carry ten pairs of copper wire which would make possible the transmission of radio signals for the CBC as well as meeting our own requirements.

Sixteen gang crews, each consisting of approximately 20 men and many newly recruited, were assembled and placed equidistant along the line. The senior, more experienced, men were selected as supervisors and were commonly refereed to as gang foremen. Listed among the more prominent names were Bartlett, Reid, Warren and Smith. The task was a formidable one and we had to rely on the gang foreman to get the most out of the men and get the job completed on time. In normal times the foremen and crews would have been appropriately trained, but time wouldn't permit that luxury.

My Work Life

To aid in following the production of several crews in the field, a system was introduced which required each foreman to submit a weekly number of swamp fictures constructed, number of cross-bars and insulators installed, number of transposition brackets inserted between wires of the same pair and number of feet of wire installed.

One of my jobs was to study the reports as received and make suitable notations on the forms before Mr. Jerrett, the district plant supervisor, saw them. Levels of production varied from gang to gang depending upon the type of terrain in which they worked, and I was cognizant of that fact. However, experience showed that some gangs were more productive than others and productivity even in those days was always a concern. Not only was man-hour production a concern for us, it was a concern for the whole organization, and with that in mind the general managers office in Toronto decided to do something about it. It was decided to start with improving the quality of supervision in the several departments and with this in mind two personnel people from that office were sent to the University of Illinois in Chicago. The university had recognized the importance of effective supervision and had developed a program of intense instruction in the field. When the people returned to Toronto the general manager decided that these two supervisors would impart this knowledge to appropriate supervisors at the regional and district levels, who in turn would impart the knowledge to the employees for whom they were responsible. John Young, the Newfoundland district personnel supervisor, and I were designated to go to Toronto and absorb in three days the technique of improving the standard of supervision and manpower output.

Upon arrival back in St. John's, John, who also had responsibility for training, started courses for district staff. Some staff members thought the program was useful, others didn't, and I had the feeling that Mr. Jerrett still needed some convincing.

One day, as I was passing the open door of his office, he motioned me to come inside. He then indicated some dissatisfaction with regard to what appeared to be lack of production from the gang crew located at Red Cliff, just west of Grand Falls. He continued to show his concern and told me to prepare for a visit to the site. I made arrangements for the two of us to proceed to Grand Falls by the evening train. I also arranged accommodations and a taxi to transport us to Red Cliff site on Monday morning.

While the Red Cliff gang crew were billeted in two rented houses, all the men including the cook usually went home on Friday evening . They returned to the site ready for work which commenced at 8 a.m. on Monday. Jarrett was anxious to observe the work habits of the crew and also the demeanor of the foreman whose name I decided not to mention.

The foreman was on site at 7:30 a.m. and most of the crew had arrived. All but three were in working positions by 8 a.m. The three laggards were slow in getting their climbers on and eventually the foreman lost his patience with them. Calling them by their first names he yelled,. "Get the goddamm lead out of your asses and get up the poles and start putting on insulators. "

The men did move a little faster and now the foremen invited Jerrett and me inside for coffee. We discussed certain aspects of the work and Jerrett alluded to the three men who were somewhat tardy. He allowed that while they went to work after the foreman chastised them he doubted if they were happy workers, and perhaps outside the presence of the foremen that didn't accomplish much. After we finished our coffee our taxi driver, Frank Ford, took us back to Grand Falls and we caught the eastbound train and returned to St. John`s.

Around the middle of the week, Mr. Jerrett invited me to his office and said, " I want you to bring the gang foremen to St. John`s and give them supervisory development program training courses." I now arranged the course periods with half the men one week and the other half the next week. The gang foremen were notified. I modified the course to some extent because we were dealing with a different group of men who were operating in the field as contrasted to those operating at the district office level.

During the last two days of the course I impressed upon the men the tremendous importance of the work they were doing and the need to get the task completed on time and within budget. They would have to get the most out of their crew and one of the ways to accomplish that was to keep them as happy as possible: Make sure they understood you had their best interest at heart. Give them a pat on the back when they deserve it. And if you have to discipline a man, do it in secret.

My Work Life

As a foreman you should always ensure that the crew appreciate your concern for their well being and that of their families. I suggested when the crew returned to work on Monday morning ask how things are at home: How are the gardens growing? How did the children do in school? Are the caplin rolling in on the beaches yet? Or, how is your mother making out, I heard she wasn't feeling good last week. How is Johnnie`s arm doing? I heard he fell and broke it last week. I said to make sure they understand you have an interest in their families' welfare.

I was about to dismiss the class when Mr. Jerrett arrived. He thanked them for attending and hoped they had learned something from the process. He outlined the need to get the job done as quickly and efficiently as possible then wished them a safe weekend with their families and success with their work. When they had left, he turned to me and said, "You and I are going back to Red Cliff Monday morning and we'll observe first-hand if the cost of the course was worth it."

I made all the logistical arrangements again and Frank Ford took us to Red Cliff in his taxi arriving there at 7:30 a.m .just as the crew were returning from another weekend at home and getting ready to go to work. Most of the men were on the job before 8 a.m. but the same three guys were still slow getting ready and pretty soon they received the foreman's attention. I was holding my breath wondering how he would react and if the course had been worthwhile.

Suddenly he exploded and said, "Alright you guys, get the lead out of your asses and start climbing up that goddam pole and get to work." And then he hesitated and added, " By the way, how's your mother?"

Mr Jerrett and I turned our backs, smiled, and joined the foreman for coffee and then left for home. I followed up the main points of the program with the foremen later. Mr Jerrett was not convinced, but the work reports showed improvement as time went by and the men did get the pole line completed on time and, most important, within budget.

~ *Chapter Thirty-two* ~

My Move to Gander

When the Americans entered the Second World War and established bases at Fort Pepperrell, Gander, Harmon and Argentia, and in Labrador and Greenland, they built their own communications system. Their trans-island network utilized a pole line owned by the Department of Posts and Telegraphs. It was later rebuilt by CNT. The northern leg of the system was operated by radio. In 1954, negotiations began with the United States Air Force and Navy concerning the maintenance and operation of their communications network. In 1955, CNT was awarded a contract to upgrade, maintain and operate the USAF system across the island. Planners, engineers, construction staff were needed. A massive training program was put in place. I was taken away from my commercial position and given the task of recruiting and training adequate technical personnel to operate and maintain the inside plant sector. The Company rented space in the old Knights of Columbus building on St. Clare Avenue, and I began classroom instruction for the first 30 students I had recruited.

Very few of the students, many former employees, had a technical background. Training began in basic electrical theory and went from there. The students worked hard and after four months of intensive classroom instruction they were assigned to various repeater stations for on the job training. About 250 people were training in the different categories. I operated

My Work Life

four classes and then followed through with on the job training, which took me across the system several times. When the old system had been upgraded, and much new equipment had been installed, a new operational headquarters was established at Gander. A service center and systems stores were also established there. I was offered the position of station supervisor. I accepted the position and moved to Gander in May of 1957. The new town site was in the early stages of development and the Ministry of Transport was demolishing old buildings as they were vacated. I moved into the old Jupiter Hotel and, as quickly as I could, arranged the construction of a house. I spent seven months at the Jupiter before my house was finally ready for occupancy. Our house was the second to be occupied on Medcalf Street, the second oldest street in Gander. Memorial Drive is the oldest street.

During my time at the Jupiter, I would return home to St. John`s Friday evenings and come back to Gander on Monday. The return airfare on Trans Canada Airlines was $15.00

I`ll always remember the night when Joan and the two children finally arrived in Gander on No. 1 train from St. John`s. They arrived at 10:30 p.m. in November, in the midst of a raging snow storm.. We were quickly settled away in our new home and Brian and Betty entered school. The schools were still located at the airport site. This was not inconvenient because my office was also located on the airport. Soon the snow melted and for the rest of the fall we were up to our ankles in Medcalf Street mud. For the longest time I was required to devote day and night and most weekends to my job. As the system became organized I had my evenings free, but there were other things to do. New churches had to be built, new schools were needed, and I soon found myself involved in several community organizations. I was chairman of our Church Financial Committee, a member of the Building Committee, chairman of the Wells Foundation, member of the School Board, member of the Hockey Association, President of the Baseball League, member of the Lions Club, chairman of the Boy Scouts Committee and a member of other organizations as well.

Many other people were similarly involved and eventually the airport town of Gander took shape, a town of which we were and still are justly proud. The years passed and in 1961 the USAF decided they no longer needed the Newfoundland

My Work Life

bases and so there was no need for a communications system. The greatly diminished telecommunications requirement could be met from commercial sources and the system was phased out. The employees were all absorbed by CNT. At this time, I accepted a new position with the parent company as a testing and regulating inspector with headquarters at Gander. I was given overall responsibility for inside plant equipment in the area Eastport to Baie Verte, and the whole of the south coast.

CNT was undergoing considerable reorganization and expansion, and my new position required much travel to and from St. John`s. On one trip, returning from Gander, I shared a seat with Con Sutherland, who was the officer in charge at the Gander Weather Office, and Cyril Rowsell, the OIC at Gander Aircraft Control Center. Both were good friends and popular and influential in the community. A town council election was taking place and they persuaded me to run. I gave a commitment that if they would nominate me and actively support me, I would run. They agreed and I was elected along with John Robertson, Bill Harris, Bill Lahey, Roy Cooper, Don Blackmore and Ernest Peyton on November 14, 1961. John Robertson was elected Mayor and Bill Harris Deputy Mayor.

~ Chapter Thirty-three ~

The Jupiter Hotel

When I first moved to Gander and was staying at the Jupiter Hotel my days were very busy, beginning at 7 a.m. when I breakfasted at the terminal restaurant, then went to work. Lunch and dinner were also eaten at the terminal. The restaurant and hotel were operated by Commercial Caterers. A Mr. Dean was the manager, however it was Mrs. Manuel, assistant manager, who ran the show.

In the days of construction and modification to the USAF Communications System many people were moving in and out of the airport. Practically every night some of our people were billeted at the Jupiter. Town people would generally arrive by train, the east bound and west bound trains arriving at or around 11 p.m. The Jupiter was almost always sold out, seldom was there a vacant room. Sometimes people could not be accommodated, so the Jupiter staff would very often place a telephone call to the USAF Repeater Station to enquire if the people who had reservations were arriving.

It was a system operating practice that each and every telephone call to the station was entered into the station log. The entry showed the time of the call and the purpose for same. On occasion, Mrs. Manuel would call, but most times it would be a member of the hotel staff.

Mrs Manuel was a large and imposing woman. She was very authoritative and not reluctant to let me know what she thought of the people I had working for me. Many of my staff didn't like her very much but they were always courteous in their dealings with her.

Charlie Prim, who retired from CN at Gander, was one of several wire chiefs who at this time worked the early night shift which terminated at midnight. Sid Greeley, who later joined EPA and became famous in his own right as a pilot, was one of the wire chiefs whose shifts started at midnight. Sid was a barrel of energy and, in addition to doing a lot of work, he answered just about all the telephone calls coming into the station. The first ring of the phone and he was on the way to answer it .Charlie Prim was a prankster and always figuring ways to trick someone. He was very witty, had a good collection of stories, and could mimic anyone. He could mimic Mrs. Manuel perfectly. Charlie was boarding at the Eastbound Inn. One night, just before retiring, he decided to play a trick on Sid Greeley. He called the repeater station where the response was, "USAF Repeater Station, Greeley speaking, can I help you?"

Charlie changed his voice to resemble Mrs. Manuel and inquired if those people from St. John's for whom she was holding a room had arrived.

Sid said he would check the log and let Mrs. Manuel have the information.

Charlie did this dozens of times and Sid never did know the difference.

Finally, Charlie tired of this game so he decided to tell others and they in turn informed Sid of all the tricks he played on him. Upon being made aware of this, Sid's response was "By the lord dying (you know what) wait until that SOB calls again."

Of course, Charlie didn't call again. This night when the phone rang and the voice at the other end identified herself as Mrs. Manuel, Sid had his chance, "You goddam rotten son of a bitch," he said.

Mrs. Manuel was dumbfounded. and by the time Sid realized this was the real Mrs. Manuel, it was too late.Mrs. Manuel told him she would see to it that he would lose his job and no amount of apologizing could change her mind. The next morning I went to breakfast as usual. Before my juice arrived, Mrs. Manuel was tapping my shoulder and proceeded to let me have an earful.

She started by saying, "What kind of a bunch of animals do you have working for you?"

Before I could respond she related the whole incident. I had difficulty believing it. Sid Greeley couldn't possibly have called her all the things she claimed he did. At any rate, she wanted me to fire the guy and if I didn't she would go over me to the general manager.

I went to the office. By now Sid had gone home, his shift ended at 7 a.m. I reviewed the log and there was reference to the incident but not much detail. I telephoned Sid, who was staying at the Airlines Hotel. He answered the phone on the first ring. As soon as he heard my voice he said, "I'll be right down" and so he was. He relayed the whole story to me and it was the first time I had heard about Charlie's calls. I could understand how Sid would react as he did.

I said, "OK, you and I now are going over to see Mrs. Manuel and see if we can explain our way out of it." As much as we tried, she would have none of it and she followed up on her threat and called the general manager of CN at Toronto.

Harold Clark, a Newfoundlander from Victoria, and a former CN superintendent in Newfoundland, was the general manager. He called me right away and in typical fashion said, " Collins, what in the hell is going on down there?" He knew Mrs. Manuel and how many times we had sought her cooperation in finding accommodations for staff. He was furious. "That young Greeley fellow should be fired," he said, "I want a full investigation and a report right away."

I set up the investigation. I brought Charlie and Sid and their union representative together. I must say that even though I reprimanded them both, I had no intention of firing Sid. We had to find a way to pacify Mrs. Manuel. I left that to the three of them. They were to report back to me that day. It took more than a day, but finally the matter was resolved. When I relayed the whole story to Mr. Clark he said I was just as bad as the boys and he didn't want to ever hear of anything like that again. I was happy it was over. Mrs. Manuel has since departed, God rest her soul.

~ Chapter Thirty-four ~

Shooting My First Caribou

During my first year in Gander Bay I became very good friends with the Hurley family who subsequently moved to Glenwood, When Joan and I moved to Gander we renewed our friendship. Gilmore Hurley and I became close friends and did a lot of fishing and hunting together. In the fall of 1960 I applied for and received a caribou licence. Towards the end of September, Gilmore and I set off from Glenwood on his river boat for Northwest Gander River. We had planned to shoot a stag but realized we didn't have too much time if we were going to get a good animal. You see, the mating season starts around the end of September and a stag in rut is not good meat.

Gilmore had a cabin at the Salmon Hole near Redrock Brook at the upper end of Long Angle Island. We arrived there in time to walk back to the meadows, a distance of five or six miles. The meadow was a good place for caribou. There was herd in that general area, known as the Mount Peyton herd. We hunted that afternoon and again the next day, but saw nothing other than one or two small does. The next day, Gilmore decided we would go up river. If need be, we would go as far as Robinson`s Brook. There was a good camp there owned by the Gillinghams of Gander Bay.

There was lots of water in the river, so we loaded our things and left.

We saw plenty of game on our journey, moose, birds etc. It

My Work Life

was a sunny day and later in the afternoon , down river from Robinson`s Brook, we saw one of the most beautiful stags in Newfoundland. It was feeding on a grassy bank near the water.

For this trip I had borrowed Brett Saunders` 22 special rifle. The bullets it used were slightly smaller than the 30/30 bullet and difficult to come by but Brett let me have the 8 or 10 bullets which he had. He guaranteed me the rifle was accurate. Gilmore maneuvered the boat to within 150 yards and the boat struck a rock and became grounded and quickly swung across the tide. The noise created by things shifting in the boat caused the animal to lift its head. What a beautiful sight perfectly silhouetted against the sky background. Gilmore held the boat steady and I took aim and fired from a standing position. The caribou jumped but remained standing, still broadside to us. I put in another shell and fired again and the animal collapsed. We floated the boat and motored up to where it lay about 20 ft. from the water.

It was just about dark, so we quickly bled and paunched the animal. We took the liver and heart and left for the camp at Robinson`s Brook. It was quite cold and I was wearing wool mitts when we arrived at camp. Gilmore proceeded to fix up the stove and lit a fire. I brought our sleeping bags, food and things from the boat to the camp. Gilmore suggested that we have caribou liver for supper. Wearing my mitts, I went back to the boat and picked up the liver which was now quite clean and dry. After getting things arrange in the cabin we started to prepare supper, rendering pork fat in the pan along with onions, two staples in the country.

We had a drink to celebrate my first successful caribou kill. Then we sliced a generous portion of liver and proceeded to fry it in the pan. It didn't take long before we literally had to leave the camp. The musky odor was such as to make it impossible to breathe. We removed the liver from the camp. I didn't know what was the cause of the terrible smell, but once outside Gilmore told me. He said the stag was in rut and while the liver could be affected worse, it was likely the whole carcass would be inedible.

I was discouraged but still hopeful the meat would be unaffected.

We arranged something else for supper and went to sleep. The next morning bright and early we had breakfast and took off down river to check on the carcass to cut and clean our meat.

To our dismay, the meat was no good. The smell of it was equally as bad as the liver. Just then Olendo Gillingham, a wildlife officer, came by. The air was so pungent with that musky smell that he confirmed before he stepped from his boat what we already knew. He agreed we could leave the meat where it was. We decided we would leave the antlers until we were ready to go back to Glenwood.

My hunt was over, but all was not lost. Gilmore had a moose licence so we set out to find one. We had no luck that day. An early rise next morning found us hunting the river with out vision obscured by a dense low lying fog, not an uncommon condition in the early fall.

We soon saw two moose, a cow and what must have been her calf. We didn't want the large animal so Gilmore took aim and killed the calf. Holy hell broke loose on the river. The cow went into a rage and charged towards us. Our boat was aground and we left the boat and ran ashore and proceeded up two trees. The moose came within a few feet of the boat and retreated to the dead calf. Time and time again, with froth running from her mouth, she would charge the boat, always stopping short of contact with it. She paid little attention to us. We finally decided we would try to scare her away. There was no real danger to us because, after all, we had a gun. She remained pretty stubborn for a while but finally ran away in the woods. She did come back to the edge of the river a few minutes later, but we didn't see her again. I had never heard of a moose attacking anyone before that.

We paunched our moose and left for home. However, when we arrived where I had killed the caribou the antlers were nowhere to be found. I thought Olendo might have taken them but he claimed he didn't. Consequently I have no proof that I killed that majestic animal. Gilmore Hurley is my proof and if you want to verify these facts you may get in touch with him. He is still living with his family at Glenwood.

~ Chapter Thirty-five ~

Fishing With Larry G.

It was in the summer of 1965 and I had made many trips to Glenwood but hadn't had much luck with salmon. It was around the middle of July and I had gone to Glenwood in the evening after work. I had caught one salmon in the Upper Salmon Brook Pool and was on my way back to Gander. As I was crossing the bridge, I saw Eric Francis pass under the bridge in his boat and land in the lagoon behind the house where Olendo Gillingham used to live. I crossed the bridge and turned around at the Appleton access road and went back to ask Eric how the fishing was down river. He told me there was a good run of fish down at Petries and also at the lower end of Fourth Pond. I made arrangements there and then for him to take me down there the next day. I went home, picked whatever was necessary for the day`s trip and was looking forward to a good day`s fishing. Around 10 p.m. Eric phoned me to say he had another offer to take a party of two down river for three days, and since I was going for one day only he didn't know what to do. Realizing the importance of the three day`s income for him, I didn't hesitate to let him take the two guys for three days. He was most appreciative and told me he would try to find someone else to take me down. Sure enough, just before midnight, he called back and said he would engage a guide I'll call Larry, if that met with my approval. I had never fished with Larry but I knew his name and presumed he would be a good river man and guide. I told him to tell Larry I would be in Glenwood at daybreak.

Next morning I was out of bed early and arrived at the appointed place where Eric and Larry kept their boats. Larry was waiting for me. We put my things aboard and left for Petries Rock, which is at the upper end of Fourth Pond. Eric's boat was still on the beach and Larry told me that he would be leaving around 8 a.m. Bernard Cooke from Bishop's Falls and Ben Elliott from Botwood were the two men that Eric was taking down for three days. They were going to stay at Goodyear's cabin at the lower end of Fourth Pond.

On our way down river we passed by many people fishing from the shore. Some had walked down the side of the river as far as Long Rattle. There was a boat fishing Nut Brook but no one was at Bridget's Angle. This was a good place to fish in the morning, provided you were the first person there. Larry landed the boat. I had my rod and line ready. I made about four or five casts and hooked and landed a small grilse . We lost little time there and headed for Petries to try and get there before others might arrive. As luck should have it, no one was fishing at Petries, so we maneuvered to the best pool and anchored our boat. In little time I hooked a fine salmon and was having much fun playing it. It was not yet ready for landing when Eric arrived with Bernard Cooke and Ben Elliott. They passed by us and landed on the sandy beach below the Rattle. No sooner had their boat been beached when Bernard and Ben broke out a bottle of rum and proceeded to have a drink. They were obviously in a fun mood and we could converse with them as it was so still on the river.

As soon as Larry saw the liquor he wanted to go ashore and join them. I wasn't interested, especially since there were lots of fish jumping and finning in the water. Larry, however, exhibited a greater interest in the booze, and when I landed my fish he proceeded over my objections to pull up the anchor and go ashore.

I had know Ben and Bernard for years, so I had a drink with them, although it was rather early in the day. When our drink was gone I suggested to Larry that we return to the pool. Larry was having none of that. He wanted more liquor and to my dismay, Ben and Bernard accommodated him. After two or three drinks Larry had no intention of going back fishing. As much as I pleaded with him, it was to no avail.

Ben and Bernard began to realize that the effect of their good intentions was about to ruin my day. They instructed

Eric, their guide to push off and go on down river to their destination. Eric pulled away and Larry was hell bent on following him. I became quite firm and insisted that we go back fishing, but Larry was having none of it. Instead, he started the motor and headed for the lower end of the pond, and there wasn't a thing I could do about it.

Eric`s boat arrived at Goodyear`s cabin just ahead of us and they proceeded to carry their supplies from the boat to the cabin. Larry joined in and, in a matter of minutes, Bernard, Ben, Larry and Eric were again bending their elbows. I realized my day was ruined and I was pretty much disgusted, not only with Larry but with Bernard and Ben. I thought they should have exercised more restraint, especially insofar as Larry was concerned. Several drinks later, Larry passed out and only then did Ben realize that they had ruined my day. Around two o`clock I decided I had enough and I readied Larry's boat for the trip up river to Glenwood. By this time Larry was awake and there was no way he was taking me back to Glenwood. His plan was to stay overnight with Ben and Bernard and I could get back to Glenwood by any means, but not with him. At this stage my patience was exhausted, and I grabbed Larry and pushed him aboard the boat. I pushed the boat off from the beach and started the motor. Larry- persisted in making a nuisance of himself and came back in the boat towards me. I I took the pole and held it over his head and told him to lie down in the head of the boat otherwise I would knock him over with the pole. I was prepared for a real battle with him, but to my delight and surprise he lay down. I started the engine and we soon motored the length of Fourth Pond.

Larry remained in the horizontal position in the head of the boat while I proceeded up river to the bottom of the Big Chute. I had never driven a boat up over the Big Chute before and I was hesitant to try it, especially with Larry onboard. I was considering what I should do when two boats from Allied cabins arrived from down river. It was Calvin Gillingham and Roland Gillingham. They were heading to Glenwood to pick up two guests for a fishing trip at Allied`s cabins. When they saw me they stopped their motors and landed. When I told them of my predicament they were inclined to awaken Larry and leave him on the beach. Instead, Calvin took my boat over the Chute and walked back and brought his own boat over. They went on their way and I proceeded towards Glenwood, staying behind the other two boats.

Calvin and Roland landed their boats on the Appleton side of the river just past the Queen Elizabeth Bridge. I landed Larry's boat at the same spot we took it from in the morning, on the other side of the river. My car was parked just a few feet away.

Larry moved around and turned over, an indication he was still alive. I took my rod and bag, put it in the car and was about to pull away when Larry's wife arrived on the scene. She was in a bad mood when she arrived and seeing Larry's condition it triggered something within her. She was very vocal, cursing and threatening him. Whatever it was, Larry got the message, and soon became vertical and left the scene. My car engine was already running and I quickly cleared off the beach. I drove to the Trans Canada Highway, overlooking the beach where Larry's boat was.

Larry's wife had picked up a piece of driftwood and was giving every indication that she intended to beat up the boat and engine. Suddenly she looked up and saw me and started to come in my direction. I had enough for one day, so I put my car in drive and left for Gander. My wife was quite surprised that I returned so early in the day. When I told her what had happened, she seemed relieved I was home.

When Eric Francis had called on the previous night he told me Larry's rate for himself and the boat was $30 per day. In my considered opinion, Larry's performance didn't warrant any pay. In fact, I thought Larry owed me something as compensation for the grief he had caused me. I didn't pay him. After a couple of weeks, he called me. He said he hadn't been paid for the trip and he wanted his money right away. I laughed at him and told him I was sending him a bill for bringing him home. The next night I received another call and he said that unless I paid him immediately he was going to refer the matter to the RCMP. He said, " Not only did you not pay me but you ruined my engine, it was all beaten up."

I immediately concluded that after I left the scene his wife must have used the piece of wood she picked up on the motor and I told him so and then I said, "If you ever call me again I'll be out and will bring the RCMP with me."

I never heard from him again. I was concerned that I might be blamed for the damage to the engine but I found some people who had seen his wife doing the job on it. Two months passed by and I visited Eric Francis. I knew Larry's family

My Work Life

could use the money, so to ease my conscience I gave Eric $30 and he hand delivered it to Larry's wife. I trust she put it to good use. I saw Larry once or twice after that. He was pretty abusive, so our conversations were short. Needless to say, I never again engaged him to take me fishing. However, I did come close to meeting him again.

In the 1966 general provincial election, John Lundrigan was my campaign manager. About mid way through the campaign, the election committee decided I would have to do more door to door campaigning. On this morning, I was to start at Glenwood. The procedure would be as follows: Lundrigan would accompany me and he would ring the door bells. When the door was answered, John would greet the person, introduce himself, and tell them what he was doing and then introduce me. As I was talking he would go on to the next door and repeat the procedure. I had some objection because I knew the people in Glenwood and didn't need to be introduced. However, that's the way it was set up and John intended to follow the rules. We did five or six houses and everything was going fine when we came to Larry's house. I said, " John, we won't go in there."

"Oh yes, we will," he retorted.

I said, "No, we had better skip that house," but John was not about to listen. Before I could explain things to him he had started up the lane towards Larry's house. I went back to the car and sat in the driver's seat. John knocked on the front door and there was no response. I breathed a sigh of relief and expected John to return to the car. Instead, he went around to the back door. Suddenly it was as if all hell had broken loose. When John reappeared from behind the house, he was backing up with his two hands over his head as if he were pushing himself back. Larry was close to him with an axe he obviously was using to chop wood. He was giving Lundrigan a hellish tongue lashing, and John's only response to him was, " What, did you hit your thumb?"

He tried to tell Larry he was working with me, thinking that might help, but that only had the effect of inflaming an already bad situation.

Larry said, "Get off my goddam property or I'll hit you," and at the same time he saw me parked in the car. He lost interest in John and started in my direction. I had the car in gear and departed the scene before he reached the road.

Shortly afterwards, I picked John up in the upper end of Glenwood and he was still as white as a ghost. "My god" he said "what is it between you and Mr. G"?

I replied, "The next time I tell you we shouldn't visit a certain house, please believe me."

He allowed he would. Later I told him about the fishing trip down Gander River last year. He then understood.

Part of the door to door campaign procedure was identification of the voter. They were also classified as to voting habits. After each interview John would enter "PC" or "Liberal" after the name. We could generally determine how they would vote. I told him to mark Larry as "doubtful."

~ Chapter Thirty-six ~

Caribou Hunting: Wall's Pond

One day in September 1963, George Turner, whom I had come to know through building our new church in Gander, enquired whether I would be interested in a caribou hunting trip.

He said he had a trip lined up to fly to Wall`s Pond, behind Mount Peyton, and he was going to stay in an old cabin once owned by Edgar Baird.. I checked my schedule and agreed to go. It turned out George had arranged with Sam Blandford, who was the co-owner of a Cee Bee aircraft, to fly us in. He had also received the OK to use the cabin belonging to Edgar Baird. He told me I would need to take along only food and a sleeping bag.

We left Gander just before lunch and in no time were landed in Wall`s Pond, a strip of water about half mile long and quarter mile wide. Like most ponds it had a brook running in and a brook running out. The cabin was located on the west end, the run-in end.When we arrived we noted that some other people were already there, namely Lloyd Brown and Bill Kendall, both of Gander. Lloyd worked with Allied Aviation and was formerly from Glovertown. Bill Kendall was from St. John`s and was a radio operator at Gander. There was lots of room and we settled in together.

In addition to the cabin in which we stayed, there were two or three small sheds and a couple of boats. George and I went to a shed where mattresses were stored. We needed a mattress each for our bunks. There was a stock of mattresses about 6 ft.

high. It was here I had my first introduction to bats. When we lifted of the first mattress we exposed a wall to wall layer of bats. Certainly they were in the hundreds. We continued to remove the mattresses until we found clean ones, then we fitted our bunks. Lloyd and Bill told us they had been there for three days and had not seen a sign of caribou.

It was now mid-afternoon but still time for an evening hunt. George and I grabbed a lunch, and since Lloyd and Bill were going to the run- out end of the pond, we decided to hunt the near end, the run-in end, where they had hunted in the morning.

We walked up the brook but saw nothing. We came to a fairly large bog and we stopped as we were to enter it. While we were talking I saw a caribou walk out of the woods on the far side. It was a long distance and while I could not tell for sure, it appeared to be feeding. We were down wind but it was a long walk down the bog, and it was getting late.

I remembered an old trick some of the old fellows in Gander Bay had told me. I really didn't believe it, but I thought it was a chance to test it. I said, "George, I`m going to try to entice that caribou to come where we are rather than us go where it is."

George said, "Yeah, how do you plan to do that?"

I said, " Well, first I want you to start running back and forth and yelling to the top of your voice. At the same time I am going to climb this tree and wave a stream of white toilet paper. I've got a roll in my back pack."

I believe George was having second thoughts about having taken me with him. However, he reluctantly agreed and we both commenced our antics. It didn't take long before we got the attention of the caribou. After a few minutes it began to walk towards us. It kept coming, sometimes running. I left the toilet paper in the tree and came down to where George was. We both sat down and waited. As the animal came close we could see it was a stag. It kept coming until it was within 50 ft. and then stopped. It was a beautiful young animal and it started to run away. I killed it with the first shot. George was ecstatic, he couldn't believe his eyes. He was so excited that in the paunching and cutting process he became thoroughly covered in blood. We took a quarter each and walked back to camp. Lloyd and Bill had already returned. They were dumbfounded over our quick luck, having seen nothing themselves. George told them how I had enticed the animal to come to us. Their reply was, " Yeah, what else is new?"

George and I returned and retrieved the two remaining quarters. We cleaned up and had supper we then built a frame and hung our meat and covered the sides and roof of the frame with fly screen. This would allow the wind to circulate around but keep the flies off.

We had a drink or two that night and a four handed game of cards. It was agreed that the next morning Lloyd and Bill would go up the marsh where we had killed the caribou and we would go down the other end of the pond where they had been this evening. Next morning, we all left camp together. George and I saw nothing and returned to camp around 11a.m. We had heard some shots, but when Lloyd and Bill returned they didn't have an animal. Bill had done some shooting but missed. We had lunch and planned the afternoon hunt.

George and I decided to strike back over the barrens behind the cabin, while Lloyd and Bill still hunted the brooks. We had been walking no more than ten minutes when we saw and killed another animal. We cleaned it up and brought it back in quick order because we were so close to the cabin. We now had our two animals and the next day we went berry picking. Lloyd and Bill continued to hunt, but had no success. We were now in our third day and Lloyd and Bill in their fifth. It was agreed that if we saw a caribou we would kill it for them. The next day, they were up bright and early and went down to the pond. George and I had breakfast and went back over the barrens for more berries, and a caribou if we saw one. We found a good spot of partridgeberries and were filling our buckets when suddenly I heard George whisper, " Don't turn too fast but just look behind." There was one of the finest stags anyone could wish to see. It kept feeding and walking parallel to us and we watched. I had my 30/30 close by. Finally the stag caught our scent and it wasn't long before it started to run. I took aim and fired, and the animal really took off and quickly went out of sight behind a hill. I jumped up and ran in its direction and found it struggling in a bog. I walked up close and finished it with a shot in the head. We returned to camp and relayed the good news, and the four of us went back and brought out the caribou.

It was now noon and the wind had switched around from westerly to northeast and looked as if a storm was brewing. A

My Work Life

fine drizzle was falling. Bill Kendall was still out hunting, but we remained in camp during the afternoon.

Around 2 p.m. Bill came back and said he had seen no caribou but did run into a covey of partridge not far from camp. I had my 12 gauge shotgun with me and Bill wanted to try his luck at the partridge. As much as I liked partridge hunting, I couldn't refuse him. I had already had much luck with the rifle, so I said, "Yes, sure," gave him a handful of shells and off he went.

I went outdoors and watched him. He had two shots and I saw that the covey contained eight birds . After the second shot the birds flew away over the trees and Bill returned. He insisted he had shot straight and he came to the conclusion that the gun was no good or the shells were no good. I knew enough about partridge that if they were feeding near the camp they would be back. About an hour or so, I took the gun and strolled out to see if I could find them. Sure enough, I eyed one bird on the ground. After careful examination I saw seven or eight. I put shells in both barrels.

I started to walk towards the birds and they began to run away and at the same time get closer together, the young birds following the old ones. I could have killed them all on the ground, but that wouldn't have been very sporting. Finally, they flushed and I had two shots. I got three birds. They didn't go far before they pitched again. It wasn't long before I had six. I could easily have had the other two, but I left them to breed for the following year.

I came back to camp and hung the birds with the caribou. I went inside and had a cup of coffee. Nobody knew I had killed the birds until George went out to inspect the caribou and saw them.

Later in the afternoon the northeast wind increased in velocity, the weather turned bad, and it was obvious we were in for a real storm. That night, and all the next day and night the weather was terrible, not fit to venture outdoors. The third day, it improved a little. We had nothing to do but eat, smoke and play cards. We were rapidly running out of food and cigarettes.

Just after lunch, on the third day of the storm, I looked out the window facing the lake. There were about twenty caribou in the lake swimming towards us. I said, "Fellows, you remember the old wharf which was grounded down at the far

My Work Life

end of the pond, well, the high water resulting from the rain has floated it off and it has drifted up the pond."

They all looked at the caribou and agreed, but just for a moment. Suddenly they too realized it was caribou. As the caribou approached our side of the pond they turned left towards the brook which ran into the pond near our camp. This was Kendall`s chance to get his caribou. I suggested that he go through the woods and intercept the caribou, going up the brook. He took his 30.06 equipped with a magnificent scope and took off for the intercept point. After he had gone, I took my 30/30 and went in the same direction. While I was still in the woods he opened fire and I could hear caribou hooves in the water and on the rocks. I broke out in the brook where Bill was standing. I said, "Did you get one?" He said, "No, I must have moved my scope going through the woods."

As we were speaking, I heard a noise down stream and on looking in that direction saw this stag in full trot coming up stream towards us. " Will I shoot or not?" I asked. When he said , "Yes, " what was to be Bill`s caribou fell on the bank. Now each of us had an animal.

That night the wind went around to south, southwest and finally west. The bad weather had passed and tomorrow would be a fine day. We had a little tea left and not much else. We had no cigarettes. The next morning broke clear and sunny with a light breeze from the west blowing directly from our end of the pond to the far end.

This was a good day for Sam Blandford to pick us up and fly us home. About 9:30 a.m. we heard the drone of a small aircraft and suddenly he appeared over the hills on the far side of the pond. He circled over us and landed. The first thing we did was get a cigarette from him. He told us he would certainly have to make two or three trips. He said, " Get your things ready while I check some rabbit snares in another pond just a few minutes away."

With that, he boarded the plane, started the engine and taxied down the pond. When he got down to the far end he turned around facing us. He started his run to take off and lifted off before he reached us, but he didn't seem to be climbing as he should have. It seemed that the conditions of glassy calm pond affected his take off. At the mouth of the brook opposite our camp there were some really high fir trees. The plane hit the tops of the trees and careened in the steady at the mouth of the brook. It was a scary experience for us. We immediately rushed through the woods to see if Sam was safe.

When we arrived, there was Sam already outside the plane. He was walking around with his arms folded in front, holding his belly and bent over in a half crouch. He was hurting, but he assured us it was nothing serious. Before examining the plane we took Sam to the camp and gave him some tea. In no time he was as good as ever and we returned to the plane.

There was a large hole about 2 ft. long and 2 inches wide in the front of the hull and most of it was below the water line. The strut on the right pontoon was broken and separated from the plane. If we were going to repair the plane we would have to get it out of the lagoon.

The Cee Bee is really a flying boat. The wings are attached to the hull. The front of the hull, which floats in the water, is shaped like a boat. Pontoons are attached to the bottom of the tip of each wing. They are attached by means of a strut and act as stabilizers to keep the hull upright in the water and the wings out of the water.

With ropes and sticks of wood we managed to get the Cee Bee out of the lagoon. The engine and propeller, which was mounted on the back of the wings, were intact.

To stop water from flowing in the hull, we used an old mattress. It was jammed in against the aircraft skin by small pieces of wood. We managed to secure the strut to the wing by means of nylon rope. When all was ready Sam decided to try to take off again. He would then fly back to Gander and get another plane to come for us. He taxied down to the far end of the pond, turned, heading in our direction, and started to pick up speed. He was halfway up the pond and just about to take off, when the pontoon broke and he had to abort the run. The plane was brought back to the beach. The strut was reattached to the wing and water which had leaked in through the mattress was bailed from the hull. To lighten the plane, everything that could be removed was taken away. Sam went down to the pond and tried again. This time he got her off the water but couldn't get height enough to clear the tall trees. The hull hit the trees and down he came again near the original site. Once more we rushed over to see if Sam was hurt. He was still in the cockpit.

Disgusted with the whole thing, he climbed out, unhurt. As much as we tried we were unable to remove the plane from its new position. There was nothing to do but return to camp.

My Work Life

Soon it was dark again and we spent another night with no cigarettes, not even a butt.

We cleaned some partridge and a couple of rabbits which we had caught, and with some flour which Sam had in the airplane, we made doughboys. We had a good meal, played some more cards and retired for the night.

Sam told us not to worry about anything, that tomorrow someone would be searching for us. He said he had a standing arrangement with his wife, Lizzy, that in the event he didn't return as planned she would advise his friend, Austin Garrett of Eastern Provincial Airways. He said since he had planned to be home this evening, Lizzie would be in touch with Austin. Sure enough, the following day, around 11a.m., a plane appeared overhead. Sam identified it as Austin's. In no time. he landed and sputtered and stammered at what had happened. He could see Sam`s plane when he flew over.

Austin said he could take three men and some meat on the first trip and the rest of the meat and men on the second trip. Sam, Bill and Lloyd went on the first trip. Austin returned in the afternoon, hauled Sam`s snares and took George and me and the rest of the meat to Gander.

The Ministry of Transport conducted an investigation but I don't`t know what conclusion was reached. A few days after I noticed the hull of a Cee Bee on a flat car down at the railway station. I asked who it belonged to and was told it was Sam Blandford`s, bought from Jim Collins of St. John`s. Jim operated Newfoundland Aviation. Not too long after, the flying Anglican priest, Rev. Carl Major, along with Sam and Austin, and a couple of mechanics returned to Wall`s Pond. They made temporary repairs to Sam`s plane and flew it to Gander where the hull was replaced and the plane was again airworthy. I have no doubt it ferried many more caribou, rabbits and fish from the best recreation territory in the land to the airport at Gander.

As I'm writing this, George Turner has retired and is now living in Happy Adventure. Lloyd Brown is a dispatcher with Sealand Helicopters.(He asks me if I remember the two big moose he and I saw, he said they were the two biggest moose in Newfoundland, so big he said we couldn`t get them all in the binoculars). The last I heard of Bill Kendall was that he was somewhere out in Western Canada. Sam Blandford now lives in Halifax and Florida. Austin Garrett is still flying and lives in Gander.

~ Chapter Thirty-seven ~

Down The Gander River With Olendo

In my early years in Gander I would always buy a moose or caribou licence, and most years I was successful in my hunts. In 1964, I didn't have much time to hunt and was unsuccessful up until Christmas. During Christmas week I had occasion to meet Olendo Gillingham, my good friend from Gander Bay. He asked if I had a moose yet and when I said, "No" he said if he had known I could have gone down Gander River with him the previous day when he got his and saw more. In the meantime, he said, he still had two quarters of meat down there and would be going back to retrieve them after the Christmas celebrations. He promised to get in touch with me before he made the trip. Always a man to his word, he called me on Boxing Day and invited me to go down river with him the next day. He added the caution, "Weather permitting." He said there was some ice on the river, but we should be able to make it.

I was out to Glenwood bright and early. Olendo was ready and we left to go down river. Olendo had a small camp in Fourth Pond and that's where we headed, intending to stay overnight. We encountered some slob ice on the way, but not enough to cause any great trouble. Fourth Pond however was frozen over. The edge of the ice was at Lower Petries Run. We proceeded to the edge of the ice, pulled the river boat ashore and turned it over. We then walked to his camp, which was just a short distance away on the edge of the woods. It was a

My Work Life

small camp with a small tin stove near the end opposite the door. We did some hunting that afternoon and although we didn't see a moose we saw lots of signs and felt pretty sure we would get one the next day.

There was something special about cooking a hot meal and enjoying good chlorine free water for tea in the woods. We thoroughly enjoyed our supper that evening and settled away for the night. We both had sleeping bags, so we let the fire go out. The stove was between us at about where our shoulders were. Lendo went to sleep almost as soon as his head hit the pillow. He was one who was lulled to sleep by the sounds of the night in the woods but, as for me, I heard every sound and imagined a bear or some other creature creeping up on us. I became less uneasy in the woods as I gathered more experience.

We had left the kettle on the stove, and I was sure that something was moving the cover but in the darkness I couldn't see. I very carefully found my flashlight and aimed it at the stove, but there was nothing to be seen. At that instant all was quiet. It wasn't very long, though, before the sounds resumed. After several attempts I caught the culprit in the act. It was a small rat trying to get the cover, which was partly loose off the kettle. I woke Olendo and told him but he was unconcerned and told me to forget it and go back to sleep. I don't think he believed me at first. Even after I convinced him he still insisted I go to sleep as he was going to do. I couldn't bring myself to do that, so I sat up and waited for Mr. Rat to return. I kept the light on so he could get used to it. I got my rifle and sat waiting for him to return. Before too long I could hear him and sure enough, he jumped up on the stove. I made sure Lendo was out of the line of fire and I placed the barrel of the gun in the direction of the rat and pulled the trigger.

Holy Hell broke loose. My 30/30 made quite a noise and Olendo came to his toes. "What in hell are you doing?" he asked.

He was concerned that I had somehow inadvertently discharged the rifle. When he found the dead rat he knew it was no accident. He reassured me there was nothing to worry about, and since no more rats came around I finally drifted off to sleep. The next morning Olendo called me at the first crack of light. We had breakfast and went hunting. It was a still morning, no wind and a light snow falling. We startled several

My Work Life

moose, but didn't see them. The country side was almost all open birch and moose could see us before we saw them. We walked back and forth on the river side of the ridge but had no luck.

Olendo said we would have to go to the top of the ridge and maybe over it and he proceeded up the hill. We both had ropes around our waists in case we had to haul out the meat. Lendo was a tall man with really long legs and an accomplished woodsman. I was still an amateur, with short legs, and was easily winded. Olendo was always 15 or 20 yard ahead of me and sometimes would wait for me to catch up. He was about 20 yards ahead when he motioned to me to come quickly. I hurriedly walked in his direction, being careful to make no undue noise. He pointed to the moose, walking rather quickly towards a small patch of fir trees. I would have to shoot quickly otherwise the moose would be hidden by the trees. I was pretty quick with a gun, and I got a shot away just before the moose got in the woods. It was a small patch of woods, and like a flash the moose came out from behind the other end of the trees at full gallop. I pumped up another shell and fired, and down she comes! The distance was about 150 yards. We took our time and walked down to where the moose lay. To our dismay, I had shot two moose, the two of them behind about 100 ft apart, separated by the bunch of fir trees. My heart sank in my boots. Remember, Lendo was a wild life officer, and I wasn't sure what would happen now. I certainly thought I was shooting at the same moose and he said that he would have done the same thing. Neither of us was aware that the first moose had fallen. The worst about this, he said, is that we have to take two carcasses to the river. We paunched them both and Lendo figured the easiest was to get them out would be to leave them in one piece with the skin on. The hair on the snow would make it easier to haul. The big struggle was to get them up over the ridge. Once we had accomplished that, it was reasonably easy going downhill to the river. We quartered the meat and left the skin on for easier handling in the boat. We took part of the meat back to Glenwood that day and got the remainder the next day.

I took my carcass and Olendo reported the incident and held the other carcass. He later told me that there was nothing anyone could do or say about it, and he disposed of the other meat.

A very sad accident happened to Olendo in October 1966 when he was drowned going over Big Chute just below Glenwood on the Gander River.

~ Chapter Thirty-eight ~

My First Exposure to Politics

When I was growing up on Indian Islands in the days of Commission of Government, I don't recall party politics ever being discussed in our house. My first exposure to party politics was during my time at Sydney, Nova Scotia, and I had the feeling that my sister Muriel and brother Albert were Liberals. When my mother and father visited there, it was clear that they were both Liberal.

Politics became a central issue after I returned to Gander Bay. During the years leading up to the National Convention, it became clear that most people in Gander Bay were supporters of Joe Smallwood and Confederation and when he ran as leader of the Liberal party they followed by supporting him. Joan's parents, Joe and Kate Peckford, were Tories and made no bones about it except in the presence of customers in their store. I suppose they didn't want to differ too much when it came to business.

In 1945, the Department sent me to La Scie to recruit a suitable person from the community and train that person to become the postmaster/operator. The Department was having some difficulty finding suitable staff for that office. Sam Drover, the Newfoundland Ranger stationed at La Scie , and I got to know each other and became good friends. People applying for social assistance (then called welfare) were referred to him by the Commission of Government. Sam would then conduct an investigation and invariably he would recommend approval.

Norm Thoms owned and operated a small convenience store in the bottom of the harbour and it seemed to be the regular place for a lot of people, particularly men at about 8 or 9 p.m.. Sam and I went there one evening to a local National Convention meeting. Most of the people were Liberal supporters of Smallwood and Sam and I assumed the opposition role. It is interesting to note that when Sam retired from the Rangers he contested the riding of Trinity. His hometown of Hodges Cove was in that district. I could never understand why he did it but he ran for the Social Credit and lost.

I moved to St. John's in 1953 and became involved with the Tory party. Those were the days when Malcolm Hollett, Billy Browne and Jim Green were holding fort and they were more than pleased to welcome me onboard. In 1957, I moved to Gander and when the federal general election was called, Mr. Hollett called and requested that I give David Decker, the Tory candidate, all the help I could. David conducted a strong campaign. He had many good workers and everyone was more then optimistic until the last few days, when the Liberals realized they might be in some trouble and started a negative campaign ending with the slogan, "Don't wreck her with Decker," which was very effective. I am convinced the slogan made the difference and I never forgot the importance of a catchy slogan in future campaigns. We lost the riding of Gander Twillingate to the Liberals but John Diefenbaker did win a minority government in Ottawa.

~ *Chapter Thirty-nine* ~

Renewing Old Friendships

In 1957, the last four or five families left Indian Islands. It is ironic that they remained there to finish construction of a new federal wharf at a cost of $67,000. No sooner was the last nail driven in the plank than they all left for their new homes. The people went to many different places in Newfoundland, including Fogo Island and Lewisporte, and to the mainland. The move was brought about by the governments relocation program.

My brother, Harvey, and his wife, Vera, and their children, Yvonne, Allan, Marjorie, Florence and their youngest son, Earl, who was the last baby born on the island, moved to Lewisporte in the early fifties. Uncle Art Frampton and his wife, Floss, who was one of my god-parents, and their sons, Bert and Cliff, moved there in 1957. Others who followed were: Collins, Days, Hoddinotts, and Perrys from Perrys Island and Boones, Kindens, Roberts, Sheppards and Penneys from East Island. The Penney family consisted of Abe and Grace, and their sons, Roland, Charles, Art, Ken, and Clarence, and their daughters, Nellie, Mildred, and Elizabeth. There was also Abe's brother, Art, and his wife Effie. Art Penney and I were first cousins, my father and his mother being brother and sister. In addition to the family relationship, all the Penney boys were real close friends of mine, particularly Art and Ken.

After Joan and I and our family moved to Gander in 1957 and soon as the Trans Canada Highway became passable, we visited Lewisporte quite frequently and I was able to renew

My Work Life

many old friendships. Often my work took me to Lewisporte and we would combine it with social visits. We just dropped in and if it was meal time another setting would be added to the table.

One night in March 1961 I had dropped in on the Penneys and we had a great game of cards when Art and Ken asked if I would be interested in going back to Indian Islands on a duck hunting trip.

Of course, I jumped at the offer. We did a lot of hunting together before I left the island and the prospect of re-living that experience really appealed to me as they knew it would.

"We have already been out there once this spring," Art said, adding they had left a rowboat at Farewell in the event they made another trip. Art was a captain with Marine Atlantic and Ken was teaching school. Before I left to return home it was agreed that they would set the date and give me notice when I would join them.

It was late March when I got the call that the trip was planned for the next weekend, and since there was no causeway yet across Gander Bay I drove to Lewisporte. Ken outlined the overall plan. We were to take our cars by road to Farewell then we would row to Stag Harbour and stay there Friday night. Ken was married to Marie Kinden and her parents, Nath and Effie, had relocated to Stag Harbour. Arrangements had already been made for us to stay with them Friday night and go eider duck hunting from there. We had to row against a nice breeze of easterly wind and were thoroughly soaked and a little cold when we arrived at Stag Harbour just as it was getting dark. We removed our guns from the boat and proceeded to Nath`s house. Effie had a big supper cooked and after we all had a drink of black rum we had a feast of a supper. We had removed our wet clothes and they were hung by the stove to dry. The evening soon passed and we went to bed about 11 p.m. Ken set an old Westclox to alarm at 2 a.m. so it seemed but a minute we were asleep. After a quick breakfast we fetched out guns and walked to the wharf. We baled the boat and with Art on the front paddles and me in second seat we started out across Stag Harbour Run. We soon reached Shoal Point, the eastern end of Perry`s Island. I let Ken take my seat and we proceeded across the Bight to the east end of Blundon`s Island. From there, we proceeded to Short Point on the east end of Indian Island and then to Black Rock and on to Grammars Island and The Shambles.

The Shambles was similar in shape to the Shag Rocks off Cavendish in Trinity Bay, with one important difference. The Shambles rock was worn smooth with the continuing pounding of the sea and ice and was the prime spot for shooting ducks. But since it was on the outside of Indian Islands it was exposed to the northeastern winds and on many mornings it was inaccessible. When we lived on the islands, crews would almost kill to get on the Shambles.

When we arrived there was some sea caused by the previous days easterly winds, but with the wind now from the south west we figured we would have a good morning. It was pre-arranged that Ken was to stay in the boat and Art and I were to be the gunners ashore. Ken took control of the bow paddles, while Art and I took positions in the stern. There was always a period of two or three minutes between the rolling swells and when the opportunity presented itself, Ken backed the boat near the side of the rock and Art jumped to safety. Before I could jump, the seas become rough again and Ken was forced to pull the boat away. When the next opportunity presented itself Ken backed the boat in again and I jumped safely to the rock and Ken pulled away a safe distance. It was still dark but Art and I knew where we would go. He set up on the west end of the rock and I would take the east end, generally the prime berth. It was very kind of him to let me have the best berth and no doubt it was out of consideration for the fact that I hadn't had the opportunity to do this for many years.

The Shambles is about one hundred feet long and there were no blinds as such. One either sat down or lay down and remained motionless when the birds were approaching. I found sitting most uncomfortable since my backside was still somewhat sore from the sail mast hole I was sitting on in the boat the previous day. Ken moored the five or six decoys which Nath had loaned us and then left the scene for cover behind nearby Grammars Island.

Most birds are very active in the early morning and eider ducks are no exception. At the first crack of light they begin to fly and the main reason the Shambles was such a good birding spot was that it was on the flight path for birds going north in the spring. As dawn began to break, Art and I were prepared for a lot of activity. I was using my Spanish double barrel side by side 12 gauge. There was no choke on the right barrel but the left barrel was fully choked. You could almost shut your eyes and get a bird with the right barrel. With the left, the shot carried further but one had to be extremely accurate.

Decoys were used to attract the birds but all shooting was directed at the birds on the wing. Our motto was "give the birds a chance." All at once Art called."Get down." I was standing up and soon collapsed to a lying position. Two ducks were approaching from the east and were soon in range. Art said he would take the first one and told me to take the drake, which was about ten feet behind. We both fired but the birds kept going towards Stag Harbour Run. In no time at all, a flock of ten or twelve birds approached and came right over the decoys. Art fired first and I emptied both barrels but no birds fell. We both checked our shells because we couldn't believe that we had missed again.

Ken came by in the boat wondering what was going on and said that if our shooting didn't improve one of us would have to take the boat, otherwise he felt we would be going back to Lewisporte with no birds. I guess that shook us up and our shooting soon improved. I then volunteered to take the boat and let Ken try his luck.

In a while the shooting was over and no more birds flying. We proceeded to retrieve the decoys and head back to Stag Harbour. We had 15 or 16 birds and that was enough. After breakfast at Effie's we strolled around Stag Harbour, meeting some of our old friends who had relocated from the islands and sooner than we wanted we had to prepare for our trip back to Farewell and home to Lewisporte and Gander.

~ Chapter Forty ~

Politics

In 1962, a provincial general election was announced and I was encouraged to contest the Gander seat for the Progressive Conservatives. I considered the request very carefully. I had just moved to a new job with CNT and had a wife and four children to support. This had to be my first responsibility. Joan and I thought about it overnight and she said, "If you think you should do it and you want to do it go ahead. I'm sure things will turn out alright."

For me, politics had become like a religion. A meeting was arranged at my house and was attended by Gil Wells, vice principal of the school, Jim Candow, a fellow employee at CNT, Jack Hewitt and Charlie Power, both Customs and Immigration employees, Jack Burden, a self employed professional engineer, and North Kirby, office administrator of Allied Aviation. Kay Kattenbush was nominated as campaign manager and these people formed the nucleus of the organization. The next day Mac Campbell, a CBC radio reporter, joined the group as public relations specialist.

As the campaign proceeded, I sensed we were doing really well and it looked as if we could win the seat. Two weeks into the campaign, I was requested to attend a workers meeting taking place at Hotel Gander. I was a bit disappointed when I learned we were getting very little support from the provincial PC association. We were told that we could expect no more than $400 in finances and practically no support in terms of leader's visits. I understood what was happening. Resources were scarce and the provincial group were using the scarce resources in what they considered the most promising riding. I told our crew we would have to find the necessary resources in our own district and that is exactly what we did.

One election protocol required the candidate to visit the various clergy and business establishments. I was received by all of these people very cordially and was rather surprised later in the campaign when some businessmen telephoned me and requested I refrain from returning to their places of business. I had my own suspicions what was happening and they later told me they had received threats of beer license cancelling and welfare order cancellations if I was seen visiting their stores again. Naturally, I suspended further visits.

Many threats were received by phone, including warnings about travel across the Exploits and Gander river bridges. I didn't take it too serious but our people insisted that someone accompany me on all trips. I'm happy to report that nothing really happened. It was said the only laws protecting Tory candidates were the small game laws.

On polling day, I visited all the polling stations in the district and found everything in order with the exception of two station. In one, the Liberal candidate posters were conveniently displayed on the actual polling booth . In the other, the returning officer would not permit me to enter the polling station. Both of these infractions were reported to the District Returning Officer and satisfactory action was taken. I then returned to headquarters and to my home, where we waited for the results to come in. It was a close battle all evening and it appeared as if I would be the winner. Later on as the counts from Botwood came in the Liberals took the lead and won. The final count was Abbott Liberal 2,069 and Collins PC 1,841, a difference of 228 votes. The defeat rested heavy on my shoulders. I took the next day off, licked my wounds and went back to work with CNT resolving to fight again another day.

Back in Gander, I continued my term as a town councillor and contested the town council elections again in 1965 when I was successful and polled the second highest number of votes. John Robertson led the poll by the narrowest of margins and was elected by his fellow councillors to be Mayor. That accepted practice was thrown out the window when my fellow councillors elected Councillor Cooper, who came in third, to be Deputy Mayor. The majority of the councillors were Liberal, and I suspect party politics played a part in their decision.

I continued my political activity and was looking forward to the next general election. The Liberals knew they were in some trouble in Gander District and when the next election was called it was a whole new ball game. B.J. Abbott was moved to Bonavista North and Charlie Granger was brought back from Ottawa to contest the Gander provincial seat. He was made Minister of Labrador Affairs to add stature to his candidacy. Smallwood had the issue of Term 29 and was involved in a real battle with Prime Minister Diefenbaker. It was the best possible issue that could have been presented to him.

John Lundrigan, who was now teaching school in Gander, became my campaign manager. We put on a decent campaign, but it was obvious from the start that we would have a real battle on our hands. Dr. Noel Murphy was the leader of our party and, for all practical purposes, there was no provincial campaign. In fact, the provincial effort was nothing short of confusion. Dr. Murphy was defeated in his own riding, though he had been Leader of the Opposition for a full term.

When the final count was in on polling day, it was Granger 3,180, Collins 2,022.

In the fall of 1967, Jack Pickersgill, federal Minister of Transport, and Newfoundland's minister in the federal cabinet, resigned. He became chairman of the Canadian Transport Commission. His resignation caused a vacancy in the Federal seat of Bonavista- Twillingate. A by-election was quickly called to fill that vacancy and the election date was set for November 6. Charlie Granger resigned his Gander District provincial seat and became the Liberal candidate for the federal riding. Smallwood then selected and appointed Jack Robertson, the Mayor of Gander, to be the Liberal candidate in the by-election called for October 20 to fill the vacancy created by Granger's resignation.

Smallwood was a master at playing "musical chairs," but the people of Gander were totally disgusted because of the manner in which they were being used. Jack Robertson was a popular man and a popular mayor, although some of the glitter was beginning to wear off his mantle. Gander Liberals

My Political Life

were ecstatic when Jack's candidacy was announced. They were convinced it was merely an anointment. I believe Jack also thought he was a shoe-in.

With the defeat of Dr. Noel Murphy in the general election of 1966, a leadership convention had been held. Gerry Ottenheimer was elected party leader and was now the Leader of the Opposition. John Carter was president of the party. I immediately contacted Ottenheimer and said I was ready and wanted to run and win. Gerry wasn't so sure. John Carter, who was vacationing in the Carribean, returned to St. John's, and I was approached to step aside. His argument was that we now had a new and successful leader in place. A new provincial executive had been elected and a new image was emerging. They certainly didn't want a two time loser like me to tarnish that image. I had two choices, step down gracefully or fight. I decided to discuss it with my family. Overnight, we decided I had put too much into the party to be pushed aside. I decided to fight. Ambrose Peddle, who had been elected as the MHA for Grand Falls-Windsor in 1962 was defeated in 1966. The party brass decided Ambrose should contest the Gander election. Anyone who knew anything about politics knew this would be tantamount to committing suicide. Coming from Grand Falls he would never be able to bridge the gap of dissension which existed between the two communities. Furthermore, we would be accused of parachuting in a candidate. He wouldn't have a chance against Jack Robertson. I pleaded with Gerry and John to abandon that idea. Many of my supporters also made their views known and the idea of Ambrose Peddle being the candidate was dropped. The St. John's party people then contacted John Lundrigan, who had since left Gander and was now an associate professor at Memorial University. John agreed to contest the seat and come to Gander to measure his support and endeavor to get me to step aside. I told John I had no intention of doing that, and so the stage was set for a nomination committee. I set about mustering support and after a day or two there was no doubt in my mind who would win the nomination. It was the first nomination meeting for candidate selection which our party had held. Much interest was created, not only in Gander, but throughout the province.

Dr. Tom Farrell led a group from Corner Brook. While they would be ineligible to vote at the meeting, they campaigned for delegate support for me. Supporters from Grand Falls,

Lewisporte and other towns followed suit. They came for two reasons. They didn't appreciate the high handed approach and tactics of the St. John`s hierarchy and they didn't like to see me muscled out after all I had given to the party. The nomination meeting was scheduled to take place in St. Martin`s Parish Hall in Gander. It was a new building which my good friends Bill Kane, Rev. John Moss and I had built. Wasn't it ironic that the political party I had put my neck on the line for was now trying to get rid of me in my own building, so to speak?

Rev. John Moss was livid and he too did his part to ensure I was not thrown to the wolves. At the appointed time, the meeting was called to order. The chairman called for nominations. John Lundrigan was nominated by one of his fellow teachers, Heber Roberts. I was nominated by Gil Wells, who was Mr. Conservative in Gander and John`s former principal at Gander Academy.

It soon became clear that the vast majority of people in the hall were my supporters. The St. John`s people who were present quickly realized this fact. A hurried conference with John was arranged and before balloting was to begin, John gracefully withdrew from the race.

We all joined forces and fought the enemy we were supposed to fight, the Liberals. The controversy over the selection of a candidate and the nominating meeting had grabbed the attention of the St. John`s press. From that point the campaign took on provincial dimensions.

To his credit, Gerry Ottenheimer worked like a Trojan. He and his wife, Alma, moved to Gander and stayed for the duration of the campaign. Their presence and hard work contributed in no small way to my success, and I will be ever grateful to both of them. We recruited Fraser Lush, a Gander native then working as a reporter with Robinson Blackmore, to be the campaign manager. A slick canvassing and polling day organization was put in place. I started a door to door campaign and visited every house in Bishop`s Falls, Botwood, Northern Arm, Peterview, Glenwood, Appleton and Gander. The district has since been split with Glenwood, Appleton and Gander representing the District of Gander. The remaining towns comprise the District of Exploits.

My daily schedule was from 7 a.m. to 11 p.m. Towards the end of the campaign, I was almost obliged to crawl rather than walk. I lost 20 pounds in two weeks. Jack Robertson was a dyed in the wool Liberal. He was a great admirer of Smallwood. Above all, he was a popular man in Gander, and I knew I would have to be careful in any statement about him. He was a novice at party politics and his inexperience soon became evident. He inadvertently presented me with two or three issues which I used to good advantage.

In his first public statement he said, "The people of Gander should be concerned about where their member sat in the House of Assembly. Would they prefer a member who would sit in opposition with the three members from St. John's or would they prefer their member to sit with the Government?"– the implication being he would get more for his district as a government member.

I pounced on that statement and said, "The people of Gander are more interested in where their member will stand, not where he will sit." That statement was a headline grabber and from there on we started to roll.

Early in the campaign the St. John's Evening Telegram called for an interview as they were going to publish feature articles on Jack and I. The reporter arrived at our house just after supper. Towards the end of the interview, he asked how I had decided to run against Jack.

He said, "You both are good friends and are serving on council together."

My immediate response was that I was disappointed Jack did not run for our party. Had he run for us, I said, I would have been his campaign manager. That statement received wide publicity and portrayed me putting the party and community above my personal interests.

Perhaps the single most important issue during the campaign was Jack's refusal to debate with me on television. Mike Roberts, the manager of CJCN Television, the CJON station in Central Newfoundland, tried to arrange the debate. Roberts was to be the host interviewer. I agreed and I understand Jack did too. The debate was to take place at 7:15 p.m. immediately following the evening newscast. I departed for Grand Falls early and arrived there at 6:45 p.m. I needed some time to prepare for the interview, I also wanted to have some input into the seating arrangements. Jack had not put in an appearance at 7 p.m., and we all sensed maybe he wasn't coming. Soon it was suggested that we should cancel the show. I was having no part of that and insisted that the show go ahead. At 7:15 p.m. we went on live television. Mike Roberts sat in one chair, I sat in another at his right. The third chair at his left was for Jack, but it was vacant. Again, at my insistence, the cameraman, who I thought was a bit sympathetic to me, put the camera on the vacant chair every time I referred to Jack by name. It had a devastating effect on the viewing audience.

On sensing Jack would not appear, members of my staff made a hurried sign with Jack`s name on it which was placed on the chair assigned to him. Coming so soon after Jack made the statement about voters` interest in where their member sat, the vacant chair had a double whammy effect. I think Jack lost a lot of support because he was absent. I had a good interview and no one refuted anything I said.

From the time Smallwood blew the whistle until the campaign ended, Jack and the Liberal wheels were confident of winning. The man in the street knew different. Our door to door campaign was paying dividends. I worked day and night, whereas Jack`s day ended at 5 p.m. We had hundreds of workers. Twice a week the campaign workers were brought together. We told them we had a good chance to win but only if everyone worked hard. We inspired them with the challenge. They had a great opportunity to make a political breakthrough, a great opportunity to make history and bring about the beginning of a change in government in our province. It turned out the challenge was realistic and the success of that campaign was the fore runner of the change which took place in the next election.

The chief issues in the campaign were (1) the Liberal record of broken promises and (2) changing candidates in three successive elections meant that people felt they were being taken for granted.

In the general election of 1966, when Granger won the district, Gander was promised a youth center and nothing was done. Glenwood was promised paving, nothing was done. Botwood was promised that an access road from the Trans Canada Highway to the town would be upgraded and paved, nothing was done. Northern Arm was promised a telephone service, but a good pair of lungs was the only way to carry on a neighbourly conversation there.

Being slammed daily with this broken promises record, Smallwood knew his candidate was in trouble. He came to

Gander to rescue Robertson. He campaigned in his usual way. He knew two ways to campaign, promises and threats. The promises he made and did not keep were hanging around his candidate's neck, so he elected to try threats.

He told Gander voters, "It was in Gander District that I launched my campaign for confederation. It was in Gander District that confederation was born. Do you really believe sincerely in your heart that it would be good for Gander District to become the fourth Tory District with your member sitting with three members from the East End of St. John's? If you do, then it is your solemn duty to join the Tories of the East End of St. John's and vote to make Gander District part of the tiny St. John's East Tory stronghold."

The next day the paving machines were brought into action. I recall warning people to remain indoors because they were taking a chance of being buried alive in hot asphalt if they ventured out. So intense was the paving activity in Glenwood, Botwood and Peterview that anything that didn't move was paved. After polling day, the equipment all moved out.

Our campaign organization was the best that could be put together. We missed no tricks. Through a legislative change in the Election Act, Memorial University students were permitted to vote on campus through the establishment of a special polling booth. The government of the day thought it would work to their advantage but how mistaken they were. Our workers at the university asked if we would bring them to Gander for a weekend of campaigning. We readily agreed. Six bus loads of students, mainly from Gander, but many from other districts, arrived Friday evening and campaigned Saturday. We returned them to university Sunday afternoon. They were among the best campaigners any candidate could have on his side.

It was a three week campaign and everything was planned to peak on polling day. That is a day of sobering thought for candidates. I started the morning at 8 a.m. and motored to Northern Arm, at the western extremity of the district, I worked my way back towards Gander. I visited every polling station and arrived at my residence at 7:30 p.m. The polls would close at 8 p.m. and I knew the results would quickly be known. We had polling captains and agents in every polling station. Along with the returning officer, they would be the first people to know the count in their poll. They were instructed to telephone our campaign headquarters as soon as the count was finalized. By this means, we knew the result well before the media could release it. In a matter of minutes we knew we had made the breakthrough. We had won. Politics would never again be the same in Newfoundland. Gander District had turned out in record numbers and had led the way.

I won every poll but one and had a majority of 805 votes over Robertson, the Liberal. In the polling station at Memorial University, we won all but four out of nearly 200 votes. The one poll which I lost was Peterview and in that one I increased my vote by 400%.

Gerald Ottenheimer, the Party Leader who worked so diligently, along with his wife, deserves much credit for the victory. John Carter, the president of the provincial association, also made a great contribution. Many others, too numerous to mention, worked hard as well to ensure victory.

The day after the election Gerry Ottenheimer said, and I quote, "The election of Harold Collins, Progressive Conservative candidate in Gander District, marks the end of politics of promises and establishes politics of principles, the days of bulldozer politics are numbered."

He was referring to the kind of politics which tries to influence people's opinion by starting paving the day before polling day and said this had happened in Glenwood and Peterview. There were heavy trucks bulldozers and tractors all over the district for the purpose of the election.

Gerry also said that he and I intended to see to it that all of these projects would be finished, and we did.

The fun and the stress of the campaign, coupled with the thrill of success, put me on a personal high. It took several days to unwind and return to normality. Polling day was on Friday, and starting the following Monday I visited all areas of the district to personally thank the people. I soon realized they had high expectations of me. Meanwhile, the federal by election was now in full swing in Bonavista-Twillingate riding, where Charles Granger, the carpet bagger as he was now being called, was the Liberal candidate. Our man was my old buddy and CNT colleague, Wilf French. I arranged additional leave of absence and waded into that campaign.

The Gander provincial by election victory was so well received in the provincial districts which made up the federal riding that I was the most popular piece of property since "sliced bread."

The party organizers took advantage of this and I campaigned vigorously during the days available to me. Some heavyweight Tories came down from Ottawa to lend a hand. The more notable ones being George Hees and Walter Dinsdale, both former Cabinet Ministers. George Hees was a former football star and could have easily made the movies. He was a big imposing, ruddy, good-looking hulk of a man, as the ladies would say.

It was directed that George and I would team up and campaign in the Eastport area. I already knew many of the people because I had campaigned there before. As we moved around from door to door, I was amazed at how well I was received and how thrilled they were over my election a few days before. Women, both old and young, would embrace and kiss me in an _expression of joy. George, not used to being ignored, was extremely disgusted and threatened to go home. I mention this merely to highlight the importance and satisfaction expressed by the people over the success of the Gander election. It was as if they had been living under the mantle of opposition and it had suddenly been lifted. Wilf French made great inroads, but didn't win, but he did lay the groundwork for John Lundrigan`s election the next year.

By the time the federal election was over, I had been without any income for six weeks. My financial position was such that I had to get back to work quickly. I returned to my old position with CNT, where I had been on leave of absence without pay. I now had some serious decisions to make. I had a good job with security at CNT, promotion prospects were excellent and many people wondered why in the hell I got involved in politics in the first place. I also had a large young family to support.

I discussed the option available to me with CNT management who were most accommodating. The House of Assembly would generally open for two months every year beginning in February. I would receive no pay until opening day when I would receive 2/3 of my sessional indemnity. The remaining 1/3 would be paid on the House closing day. The company was willing to let me continue work until the House was called to session. Then I could avail of the leave of absence provision and return to my job on the House closing. There would, of course, be other occasions when I would need time off.

I thought about it for a long time and decided to take leave of absence for the duration of elective days. In this way my company could fill my position and, I would be a full time member. As time passed, I became a full time organizer for the party, but funds were not flush, so I eventually began to sell life insurance for Mutual Life Assurance Company. My sessional pay, plus income from insurance premiums, provided me with funds to provide the minimum needs of my family.

When the new session of the House of Assembly opened, I was sworn in, then took my seat with the three Tories from St. John`s. They were Gerald Ottenheimer from St. John`s East, the Opposition Leader; Ank Murphy, St. John`s Center; and Tom Hickey, St. John`s East Extern.

Smallwood couldn't stomach my representing Gander, and he let the people know when Gerry rose to introduce me to the Assembly.

It is customary for a new member to be introduced by his leader and welcomed by all parties and members. When Gerry started the introduction he got as far as to say, I was the son of a fisherman from Indian Islands, and "up she comes" to use a Newfoundland _expression.

Smallwood was up on his feet on a point of order, and that was the extent of my introduction. Such was my introduction to that great parliamentary institution!

~ *Chapter forty-one* ~

Shooting Birds

Over the years I have been most fortunate in that I have been permitted to occasionally conduct the traditional hunt in familiar territory. My fondest memory is of one such trip which Howard Crane, Jack Burden and I made to Fogo Island in November 1969. We left Gander Friday morning, motored to Carmanville and then went to Fogo Island by ferry. We stayed at the Fogo Island motel. The ferry passes by Indian Islands and the places where I hunted in my younger days. We had arranged with Jim Decker, who had a big longliner, to take us out for a day of shooting on Saturday. During our stay at the motel the bartender, Dominic Penton, inquired if he could accompany us, and we readily agreed. Dominic said he would bring along his smaller boat and would improve our chances of success with birds because the big longliner would be too cumbersome to maneuver. We didn't get much sleep Friday night and we were over to Joe Batt`s Arm long before daylight. We left Joe Batt`s Arm right away with Dominic`s 17 foot punt with a 35 Evinrude outboard motor in tow.

We arrived at Little Fogo Island at daybreak and the eider ducks were quite plentiful. We were having no luck from the big longliner, so Dominic offered to take me in his boat. I quickly accepted his offer, but Dominic had some reservations about my seaworthiness. He wasn't aware of my background, I think he had me classified as one of those Ganderites with little knowledge of the sea. In the small boat we could move in and out of the many coves and tickles. In a very short time we had bagged a dozen eider ducks.

At about 8:30 a.m. the ducks had all disappeared and we decided to return to the longliner, which by now was four or five miles offshore. As we approached the boat we could see Howard and Jack shooting at tickle aces (kittywakes). These are good eating little birds and are attracted within range by throwing fish liver or any debris in the water.

Crane or Burden had downed a bird and they were in the process of retrieving it from the water. Crane was on the head of the boat with a large long-handled dip net trying to dip the bird. As the big longliner approached the bird, the waves from the bow would wash the bird away leaving them to turn the boat around and make another attempt. This was very time consuming and detracted from the otherwise enjoyable aspects of shooting. We boarded the boat and everybody was surprised at the number of ducks we had. Dominic was ecstatic in his praise of my shooting skills. He allowed he had never seen my match.

After lunch , we both went on deck where the fellows were still taking the occasional shot at the tickle aces, but with limited success. Jokingly, I said "When shooting tickle aces from a large longliner, much time would be saved if you fell the bird in the boat." The challenge was issued immediately- "OK Davy Crockett, show us how its done." Since I had stuck my neck out, I accepted the challenge.

I had Jim keep the longliner heading into the wind. I made sure all the guys were at my rear, behind me. As the birds came by I would wait until it was directly over the boat. I fell three or four birds and then let Crane and Burden try. Try as they would, they couldn't do it. When the birds left the scene we motored over to a spot of ground called the Hat. We used to fish there during the fall and I had fished there earlier in my life. We jigged several large codfish and then headed back to Joe Batt`s Arm. Dominic`s father plucked the birds during the night. The next morning we returned to Dominic`s where we picked up our birds, paid Mr. Penton, gave Dominic all our rain wear, and then left for Gander. I felt satisfied for another year.

~ Chapter Forty-two ~

Tales From My Days In The House of Assembly

I am not sure if he was speaking in the debate on the address in reply to the Speech from the Throne, or if he was speaking in the budget debate, but Alex Hickman, who was then Minister of Justice and MHA for Grand Bank, made an impassioned plea that the "Grace Boehner" should be purchased and placed in Grand Bank as a museum in honour of the finest fishermen of Newfoundland and Labrador. The "Grace Boehner" was built in Nova Scotia and had been used as a banking schooner fishing on the Grand Banks. In later years, the vessel was used in the freighting service around coastal Newfoundland. It was now about to be purchased by someone in the United States to be converted to a floating restaurant.

Alex made a fine speech and most of us were touched by it. If you want to tug on the heart strings of a Newfoundlander there is no better topic than the romance of a schooner and the sea. Throw in the Thornhills and the Grand Bank fishery and you really have a tear jerker and that`s just what Alex did. Smallwood realized this and his ego was such he just had to out perform Alex. When Alex finished, Smallwood started. Instead of following through on Alex`s theme he got carried away and resurrected the infamous fishing admirals of the bad old days. During his speech he also talked about Lord Rodney, a naval governor. Rodney must have been one of his favourites, and he mentioned that he was so popular a street in

St. John`s was named in his honor. I was seated just twelve feet opposite him and I remarked, "Yes. I know all about it, I live there." I was then living at and owned, 4 Rodney Street.

"Oh yes," said Smallwood, " the Honorable Member for Gander knows everything."

He could never tolerate my speaking. He ranted and raved on and on, and he began to lecture us all on the great ships of Newfoundland.

Ships came in classes, he said, to wit, "The Venture Class, there was the Adventure, Belleventure, and – he couldn't remember the name of the third ship.

He kept repeating himself. "There was the Adventure, the Belleventure and...and."

He still couldn't recall the name of the third ship.

I said, " I know" and I did.

"Oh yes" he said with despise in his voice, " The Honourable Member for Gander knows everything."

I said, "I know, but I`m not telling you."

Of course, the name of the third ship was the Bonaventure.

He kept repeating the name of the first two in the hope his memory would be jogged into remembering the third, but no such luck.

The sweat was forming beads on his forehead and in desperation he pleaded, "Mr. Speaker, you must remember the name of the other ship."

George Clark was Speaker and he appeared to be sound asleep or completely disinterested as he didn't respond. With that rebuff, Smallwood turned to his left, where most of the Liberal members sat, and throwing up his arms, said, " Someone here must remember the name of the third ship."

Again he said, "There was the Adventure, and the Belleventure and...and."

And then Ross Barbour, who was the only one awake by this time, said "Premier, would it be the Baccalieu?"

Well, you could have heard a pin drop before the snickering started.

Smallwood said, "No, no Ross," and he returned to Rodney having a street named after him in St. John`s and the fishermen of Newfoundland liking him so much they named a boat after him as well, and that is true.

But many fishermen, and particularly where I come from, called these small boats punts as well. I couldn't resist the

My Political Life

temptation, and I rose on a point of order. Not a popular thing to do when Smallwood was speaking. He eyed me for a minute and finally took his seat.

I said, " Mr. Speaker, the Premier has given us the derivation of the term rodney. I wonder, when he resumes his speech, if he would tell the House about the derivation of the term punt."

Well, up she comes!

That got the Honourable Members awake in a hurry, and I got a real tongue lashing. The scathing was such that Tom Hickey, my colleague from St. John`s East Extern, defended me. In doing so, Tom was ejected from the House for a period of three days.

Gerry Ottenheimer was a very dear friend of mine. He was an able leader liked by everyone. After my election in 1967, he and I visited every nook and cranny of the province and I made sure he was exposed to the people and the problems which they faced in their communities. He was equally at home on a stage head in Leading Tickle or on a stage at the Arts and Culture Centre in St. John`s. He was instrumental in having me appointed Party Organizer for the province. We got on very well together. From Port au Port peninsula to Fogo Island he could always be relied on to rally the troops. To say I was saddened when he resigned as Leader in 1970 is an under statement. I was totally shocked when he also resigned his seat in the district of St. John`s East.

After several meetings, Tom Hickey and I agreed that Ank Murphy would become Leader of the Opposition in the House of Assembly. The P.C. Party also agreed that Bill Marshall who was the Party President would become the interim Party Leader and would serve until such time as a convention was held and a new leader elected. Meanwhile, Frank Moores the MP for Bonavista-Trinity-Conception, had resigned his seat in Ottawa and was beginning to campaign for the leadership of the provincial party. Smallwood, in a sly way, thought he would like to get Moores in the House of Assembly as soon as possible and he quickly called a by-election in St. John`s East and challenged Moores to run there. Frank was having none of it, preferring to conduct his leadership campaign from the outside of the House. The good people of St. John`s East chose Bill Marshall for their candidate and he was elected and joined Ank, Tom and myself in the opposition.

When the House of Assembly reopened in the winter, the opposition numbers were restored to four. Since there were just four of us, we all had front row seats, just "two sword lengths" across the floor from Messrs Smallwood, Curtis, and Rowe et al. They occupied the government benches but their time was running out.

It was early in the session when John Crosbie, Clyde Wells, Gerry Mryden and Beaton Abbott deserted the troubled Liberal Ship and moved across the House and sat on our immediate right. They became known as the reformers, having left Smallwood's government over the bridge financing arrangement with John Shaheen and the Come By Chance Oil Refinery.

Alex Hickman and Val Earl crossed the floor later on and they both joined our caucus. Eventually, Clyde Wells left the group but did not resign from the Liberal Party. Gerry Mryden and Beaton did not seek re-election and John Crosbie joined our caucus.

The Legislature Session was one of the most acrimonious in Newfoundland history. In an effort to get the budget approved and the session over with, the Liberals decided on morning and evening sittings. Normally the House sat from 3 to 6 p.m. daily. The new schedule was set from 10 a.m. to 1 p.m. and 3 p.m. until 6 p.m. and again from 8 p.m. until midnight or later, depending upon the rate of progress. Tempers were running high and insults were flung back and forth.

During the debate on the estimates for the Department of Municipal Affairs and Housing, much time was spent on the lack of housing and the quality of housing, particularly in the downtown areas of St. John`s.

Members on our side of the house , particularly the lawyers, were accused of owning and renting sub standard housing and were often referred to as "slum landlords".

Bill Marshall was speaking in the debate on the estimates in the afternoon of May 21, 1971, when the speaker left the chair at 6 p. m. When the house resumed sitting at 8 p.m. Mr. Marshall resumed the debate as per the rules of the house. On the way back to Confederation Building, he was handed a copy of a new newspaper named "The Alternate Press." The paper was started by a group of university students who had been successful in obtaining a federal grant under the auspices of the Federal Government's Opportunities for Youth

Program. The lead story in that first issue made reference to the debate on housing and carried a list of slum landlords in St. John's. Mrs J. R. Smallwood's name was among those names included in the list. As Bill Marshall resumed his speech he waved the Alternate Press he was holding in his hands, so that everyone could see it and he proceeded to read the article on Slum Landlords. He read the list and mentioned Mrs. Smallwood's name.

In the House of Commons in Great Britain, which is the Mother of Parliaments as well as all Canadian legislatures, the government members sit on the Speaker's right. In Newfoundland, the government members sit on Mr. Speaker's left. This anomaly exists in Newfoundland because when the legislature was sitting in the Colonial Building on Military Road in St. John's the most comfortable and warmest seats were on the left of the Speaker. A huge fireplace was located on that side and the government decided it would not deprive itself of that comfort so tradition be damned. The precedent had been established and when the legislature was relocated to the new confederation building the practice was continued on the ninth floor of the Confederation Building where the legislature was located. The members' washrooms were located on the opposite side of the room, thus when government members had occasion to use the washrooms they were required to cross the floor in front of the Speaker or walk around behind the curtains and the Spearer's chair. When Bill Smallwood, the Premier's son and member for Green Bay, left his seat and crossed the House, I assumed he was heading for the washrooms. How wrong I was. He suddenly turned towards our benches and smashed a solid left hand blow to Bill Marshall's head. He was about to land another blow when I jumped up and grabbed him. I held him rather firmly with my hands on his biceps and proceeded to steer him back across the floor of the House to his seat. He kept telling me that I was hurting his arms and that he had nothing against me but he didn't like what Bill had said about his mother. My response was to return to my seat.

There was great confusion in the House and, unfortunately, Mr. Bert Hemmens, the Sergeant at Arms, had stepped outside. Summoned by the Speaker he quickly returned and order was restored.

As Bob Benson wrote in the Evening Telegram column on

April 2, 1985, under the heading of House Attack: "It must be said that the atmosphere in the House at the time was not unlike that at the OK Corral in Dodge City before the famed shootout between Doc Halliday and his friends and their enemies. Tense." Mr. Benson went on to say, "Sergeant at Arms Bert Hemmens, of impressive military bearing and wearing his Second World War campaign medals, left his place by the bar of the House, marched ramrod straight as a guardsman on parade, and escorted Bill Smallwood from the House."

The Premier left the House to counsel his son and they both then returned to their seats. An unrepentant Bill Smallwood said he would do the same again if Marshall made a similar comment about his mother. Finally, on a motion by Les Curtis, the Government House Leader, Bill Smallwood was expelled from the legislature for a period of one week.

But the matter didn't end there.

In those days, Smallwood had free and unhindered access to the public on the program "Conversation with the Premier" which was broadcast on radio station VOCM. During the program, he would and did hold forth on any topic he desired. In this case, he defended his son and upheld what he did and when the House resumed an angry, nasty debate ensued.

The Speaker's rulings were questioned , and when that happens decorum suffers and the two sword lengths separation of the Government and Opposition benches was not a useful deterrent to maintain proper order. Insults were hurled across the floor and pretty soon the Government used the force of its numbers and the Opposition was expelled from the House.

In the summer of 1971 all signs pointed to a general election sometime in the fall. Gerry Hill, the Liberal MHA for Labrador South, had let it be known that he would not be running again. In my few years in the House, Gerry and I became good friends. We were both life insurance underwriters. He was the manager of Confederation Life, I sold Mutual Life, and we were both losing money. Gerry had little interest in politics and wanted out. Many of the Liberal members were concerned about him leaving because they thought the electorate might interpret his departure as an indication of trouble within the Liberal party. They knew they would lose some seats and they wanted nothing to worsen their chances.

Smallwood was moving around the province during the

summer in an effort to mend fences and pass out what goodies he could. He was in Bonavista one day with Ross Barbour and as they were driving back to the Oh Happy Sight Motel from Amherst Cove, Ross said, "Premier, what are you going to do about Gerry Hill?"

Smallwood replied, "Pave it!"

~ Chapter Forty-three ~

Politicking on Fogo Island

One of my first confrontations with the Liberal government was in March 1968 when Bill 10, an Act Further to Amend the Crown Lands Act, was introduced. The title was innocuous enough. The intent raised some suspicions and very serious questions. Clause 2 of the Bill would amend section 21A of the Crown Lands Act. The Act provides for permits of occupancy of Crown Lands for a term up to one year where occupancy is for an industrial or commercial purpose, or for a hunting or fishing cabin in an area difficult to access.

The amendment would allow permits up to five years. In my opinion, that was a reasonable and sensible amendment. The objectionable clause was Clause 3, which the government was attempting to sneak in without anyone noticing it. Clause 3 would allow the Lieutenant Governor in council (Cabinet) to authorize, subject to such terms and conditions, if any, as he may direct, the grant, lease, license or transfer of the 33 foot reservation around any of the waters in the province. I saw it as a serious invasion of human rights. Such action would prohibit people from walking around a pond or a river. The intent was to create private fishing pools, expressly on the Gander River, for an American company. A friend of mine in Gander alerted me to this fact, and I raised cane. In no time every Rod and Gun Club was behind me. Every outdoor type in the province called me. There was such a flood of complaints that the Government eventually withdrew the Bill. The people of the province gave me all the credit for protecting their interests and causing this infamous piece of legislation to be withdrawn. Prior to the amendment, a Crown Land Lease could be issued for a cabin on a pond or river. The lessee was deemed as the owner and could exercise certain ownership rights, such as prohibiting trespass. However, a 33 ft. strip between highwater mark and the water was not included in the lease. This was designed to permit access by the general public, allowing people other than the lessee access to the pond or river on the 33 ft. reservation. Allied Aviation had been given a lease on an island in the Gander River and they wanted control of the 33 ft. reservation. Their request prompted the government action and, no doubt, there were other private concerns who would have benefitted also. The withdrawal of the Bill is a good demonstration of the power of the people when given full vent. The 33 ft. reservation principle remains in force today.

During the winter, spring and summer of 1968, Gerald Ottenheimer and I traveled Newfoundland extensively, speaking at different functions and organizing at provincial district level. When the election was called we went after John Lundrigan to represent our party in the District of Gander-Twillingate. John had left Gander and was an associate professor at Memorial University. He was comfortably settled away in St. John's and not easily persuaded to enter the political field did finally agree on condition that I would be his campaign manager.

In theory, I was a crackerjack at the position of campaign manager, but I had no hands on experience. I soon learned my role and John found out what was expected of a candidate.

We approached it with a lot of confidence and "piss and vinegar."One of the things I noticed about him was his handshake. He seemed to be reluctant and his grasp was something less than firm and friendly. I didn't know how to mention this to him, but I had to. When I did he was very receptive to what I had to say, which was "Wherever you see a hand hanging from an arm or a sleeve, go for it and shake it firmly and warmly."

The next day we started campaigning on New World Island, in Cottrell's Cove. He was so determined to shake people's hands that whenever a person appeared he would run towards them, sometimes scaring them. After a day or two, he became a professional and before the campaign was over he was among the best political campaigners in Canada.

We put together a great political organization. I was thrilled to be involved in a campaign again, especially against Charlie Granger. Charlie and I were good friends and he was a decent man. I used to tell him I couldn't for the life of me understand how he became a Liberal! We ran into him several times in the campaign, and I think that Charlie sensed that we were going to make it tough for him.

Several funny things happened in the campaign. I remember one afternoon on Fogo Island we were driving through Barr`d Islands. It was difficult for a goat to manoeuver over the road through that beautiful little community. We were taking our time in a large four door sedan. We had a public address system on the car and John was making his regular pitch to the voters. Howard Crane, God rest his soul, was driving. I was in the back seat giving direction and advice. It was still the custom in some places that when politicians arrived, residents would fire gun salutes. Some of the old muzzle loaders which were used for this could make quite a bang. If residents happened to be supporters they were inclined to put in bigger loads and fire more of them. Whenever John was speaking, we drove slowly. On this particular day, it was warm and he had the window down and his arm resting on the door ledge. The houses were close to the road and as we approached this one house I noticed an old fellow come out the back door with a big sealing gun and point it towards the sky. Well, when he pulled the trigger, all you could see was black smoke. The sound reverberated off the breakwater and around the community and shook the car. Crane almost ran off the road. Lundrigan put the window up and stopped speaking, convinced that the old gentleman had shot at him. I was rolling in laughter in the back seat, and it took me several minutes after Crane left the community to convince them that the man was welcoming us, and that he was in fact a supporter. I implored them to go back, which they did. They opened fire again, but this time John enjoyed it.

That same afternoon we scheduled a public meeting at Seldom. The meeting was to be held in the Orange Lodge. I knew that Seldom was pretty solid Liberal, and I didn't expect too many people to turn out. So that John would not be disheartened by a small crowd, I explained to him that most of the men were out fishing and the women would be reluctant to come out to a political meeting alone. Howard drove thought the community and John made his pitch and reminded people of the meeting and how he looked forward to seeing them there. At the appointed time, we arrived, met our local representative and proceeded inside the hall. About 30 people were already seated. In fact, they about filled the hall. We proceeded to the front where a table and some chairs were positioned on the small platform. Although I knew most of the people present I introduced myself and after a few preliminary comments introduced my good buddy, John.

John didn't make one of his better speeches. I don`t know if the shock from the muzzle loader unsettled him or what was the cause. An uncle of mine on my mother`s side, Uncle Allan Sheppard, who had relocated from Baie Verte to Seldom, was in the audience. I hadn't seen him for years and he appeared restless. I attributed his condition to the fact that he was looking forward to seeing me. He was about 75 years of age, a big strapping, healthy looking individual. John hd never seen the man before in his life.

When John finished, Uncle Allan called out, "Is that all you fellows have to say?"

When we told him it was, he said, "Well, I have something to say," and with that introduction he deftly proceeded to the stage, had us stand on one side, and if you ever heard a partisan political speech, he gave it. "Now," he said, "I hope you fellows learned something," and he wished us luck and left.

John was shaking like a leaf on a tree and Howard Crane muttered under his breath, "Who in the name of God was that"

The audience burst into loud applause and filed out.

I said, "Fellows, I`m sorry, but I didn't know he was going to do it or I would have told you."

"Yes, OK but who is he?" they asked.

I said, "He`s my uncle and it's the first time I`ve seen him in years," and I apologized for his behavior. We went over to his house after and he was getting a great kick out of it. John and he got along just fine but we wondered what effect it might have had on the people who were at the meeting. As it happened, we didn't win Seldom. But then again, we never did before, and we haven`t since. But I will tell you that John

Lundrigan won't forget Barr'd Islands and Seldom Come By, and Uncle Allan Sheppard.

We continued on with the campaign. We had a lot of fun, met a lot of people, made a host of friends. They must have seen something good in us. When the votes were counted, John Lundrigan was declared elected P.C. in Gander - Twillingate. He went to Ottawa with the famous six, the others being, Frank Moores, Ambrose Peddle, Walter Carter, James McGrath and Jack Marshall.

~ *Chapter Forty-four* ~

Frank Moores Elected

When Ank Murphy became leader of the party everyone knew it would be for a short term. Almost immediately a leadership convention was announced and seven people were contestants: Frank Moores, Hubert Kitchen, Walter Carter, Joseph Noel, Hugh Shea, F. Howard Rose and Walter Carter. I supported Frank from the start and worked very hard on his behalf. The MP`s were all supporting Walter Carter and I was under extreme pressure from them to also support Carter. I remained a Moores supporter, as did most ,if not all of our caucus, which had now increased in size by the crossing over of Earle, Hickman and Crosbie. Frank Moores was elected and became the leader of the party.

Moores ran the party from the opposition room when the House was in session. He had no seat in the Assembly. When the legislation was closed he traveled the province extensively. I had the good fortune of traveling with him on many occasions. When Smallwood finally called the election, we were ready.

In the fall of 1966, there was a general election in Newfoundland and Labrador. In the short space of a year the government party suffered a humiliating defeat in a by election in Gander, in 1968 a federal general election saw the election of six Tory MP`s, in the ensuing days the provincial cabinet split over the Come by Chance Oil Refinery financing arrangement.

Ministers John Crosbie and Clyde Wells had not only resigned from the Liberal cabinet over the matter, but crossed the House as independents. They were later joined by two other ministers, Alex Hickman and Val Earle. Gerry Myrden and B. J. Abbott, two backbenchers, joined them later. Crosbie, Hickman and Earle subsequently joined our caucus. Smallwood delayed calling the election as long as he could under the rules of the Constitution. He finally announced it for October 28th.

In Gander District, my workers were ready and eager to go. Mrs. Audrey Sampson, a live wire if there ever was one, accepted the position of campaign manager. Our party had recruited a number of new candidates across the province. In Gander, we had a seasoned political machine and this permitted me to travel to other districts and help them in their campaigning.

I traveled and did much work in the Districts of Lewisporte, Twillingate, Fogo, Bonavista North, Bonavista South, Hermitage, St. George`s, Humber Valley and Baie Verte, and White Bay South.

During that campaign, threats were made on my life, on my wife and children and on some of my supporters. Thank goodness nothing ever materialized. I had two opponents in Gander District. They were Doug Sheppard, a Liberal, and a Mr. Lingard for the NDP. Eighty-eight per cent of the Gander electorate went to the polls and the final count was: Collins 5,030; Lingard 222; Sheppard 2,861. I will never be able to adequately express my thanks to my supporters for that success because in all the election period, I spent only four days in the district. The rest of my time was spent helping others.

When the dust had settled on the night of October 28th, the political situation in Newfoundland and Labrador had never been more confused. A record 90% of the electorate had turned out and voted. They had given Frank Moores Conservatives 56% of the popular vote, but just 21 of the 42 legislature seats. Smallwood`s Liberals held 20 seats and the New Labrador Party, represented by Tom Burgess, one seat.

Although Smallwood had been defeated he clung to power. For a period of two and one half months he went on making decisions, some of them costly. The events leading up to his resignation had all the ingredients of comic opera. The

My Political Life

political stew brewing in the province was enough, as Frank Moores cracked, "To immortalize the Newfie joke."

The final outcome was hinged on wooing Tom Burgess, the burning of 105 ballots and a ruling of the Newfoundland Supreme Court. Tom Burgess, the only NLP member, became the key to the victory. If he threw his lot in with the Conservatives, which at first he said he would do, we had a clear majority. If he went with the Liberals it was all tied up, a dead heat.

In the St. Barbe South district, Ed Maynard, the Conservative candidate, had squeaked in by a majority of only 8 votes. The Liberal party demanded a recount. It was during that exercise it became known the returning officer had destroyed the 105 ballots from Sally`s Cove, one of the communities in the district. They had gone up in smoke in a wood burning stove. The case was referred to two Judges of the Supreme Court. As the Canadian Press put it, "The development of the plot kept Canada in suspense all through the winter."

In time, the two Judges ruled that the Conservatives had won St. Barbe South fair and square. This meant the count remained Conservatives 21, Liberal 20, and New Labrador Party one.

Faced with these facts, Smallwood resigned on January 17th and the Lieutenant Governor asked Frank Moores to form a government.

The drama wasn't yet over for almost immediately A.G. Oldford, the Liberal member for Fortune, resigned. That was followed by Conservative Hugh Shea joining the Liberals. He became displeased because Moores didn't offer him a Cabinet position. That left the scoreboard looking like this: Conservative 20, Liberal 20, NLP 1.

A speaker would have to be appointed from the Conservatives and could only vote in the case of a tie. With the appointment of the Speaker our numbers were reduced to 19. With these dubious figures to juggle, Frank Moores began his uneasy minority rule on March 1.

On the same day, William Saunders, the Liberal member for Carbonear, resigned. That left the House split 19/19 and two vacancies. Premier Moores immediately dissolved the Legislature after a one day sitting and a Throne Speech and announced a new election for March 24.

I was now Minister of Municipal Affairs and Housing, my first Cabinet appointment. Ed Roberts had succeeded Smallwood as Leader of the Liberal Party and he led them in the campaign.

Premier Moores called a hurried meeting and outlined the political strategy for the campaign. Several of us were assigned duties outside our own districts. I was directed to assist Alex DuNphy (St. George's), Wallace House (Humber Valley), Ed Maynard (St. Barbe South) and Bren Sullivan (White Bay South). That meant I would again be required to spend more time away from my own district. Some of my workers expressed the concern that I might be open to charges of taking the voters for granted. My response was that we had to win a majority government, and I thought the people would understand and appreciate that. My opposition this time around would be Eli Baker, Liberal, and Earl Boone, NDP.

March is not considered a good time for campaigning in Newfoundland and Labrador. Weather conditions often dictate schedule changes and a stormy polling day could be disastrous. I was campaigning in Wesleyville this day when word came from election headquarters that I was required to be at Port Saunders that night. Ed Maynard had rescheduled a rally there and I was slated as guest speaker. Because of the close vote in that district last time around, it was imperative that I attend. Arrangements were made for Gander Aviation to pick me up at Wesleyville at 2 p.m. and fly from there to the airstrip at Port aux Choix. Maynard's people would meet me there and we were to leave by car immediately for Port Saunders. The plane arrived at Wesleyville and we left for Port aux Choix at 3 p.m. – an hour later than planned. The plane was a Cessna 180 which Gander Aviation had chartered from a Quebec Airline. The pilot was also from Quebec. He spoke English but knew little of Newfoundland geography and climate.

We arrived at Port aux Choix around 5 p.m. and it was quite stormy. The Gulf ice had blocked the coast to the extent that it was difficult finding the runway, but eventually we did and landed without incident. I was wearing ankle high overshoes because until now the weather had been fine. I wore a top coat and scarf, no cap. When the plane stopped near the little shack on the end of the runway, which was near the road, I opened the door and jumped out. I went to my waist in snow. It seemed that the farther I went away from the plane the deeper the snow became. I returned to the plane and we considered what I should do. Should I take a chance that Maynard's people could reach me or should we go back to Deer Lake? We had to decide quickly as it was becoming late and the pilot wanted to return to Deer Lake before it was too late. I realized I couldn't assist Maynard at Deer Lake, so I decided to get out and hope for the best. The plane left immediately.

I started towards the road as the plane prepared for take off. The road was parallel to and near the beach with Port aux Choix a couple of miles away. The farther I got to the road the deeper the snow became, until I could scarcely move. From the air it looked like a pretty good day on the ground, but the low drifting snow was causing stormy conditions and the road was blocked. When I reached the road I stopped and it was then I realized I was in some trouble. There was no way a car could reach me, I would never be able to make Port aux Choix on foot, and darkness was fast approaching. All of a sudden, out of nowhere, I saw the headlights of a vehicle and realized as it approached it was a snowplow. As it drew near I was terrified it might run over me, but I had to stand my ground so the driver would see me. Thank God he did, and just in the nick of time. He put his window down and called out. He then opened the door and I managed to get aboard.

"My dear man, you're some lucky. Had I not come by you would have drifted over," he said, adding he was considering waiting until after supper to try and open the road to Port aux Choix but changed his mind, and it was lucky for me that he did.

It took a long time to get to Port au Choix. We finally made it and he dropped me off at Mrs. Billard's boarding house. They had difficulty believing that I flew in that afternoon and was picked up by the snowplough.

I telephoned Maynard, who was stormbound at Hawke's Bay. He had cancelled the meeting at Port Saunders for that night and rescheduled it for the next night. I dried off, had a good supper, enjoyed good company, and finally retired for the night.

The next day we drove to Port Saunders where we had a lively and enthusiastic meeting and stayed overnight. The following day, I motored to Deer Lake and flew back to Gander. I spent a couple of days in my own district and then it was off to Stephenville, where Alex Dumphy met me and I spent two days campaigning with him.

The weather had improved and campaigning was now more enjoyable. We did a lot of door to door campaigning in small, farming communities where the houses were far apart. To save time, we took the shortest possible route from one house to the next. That generally meant climbing over fences. Towards the close of the first day, I had a misfortune. Climbing over this rather high and unsteady fence I was sure I heard the sound of clothes ripping. On further investigation, I found the seat of my trousers ripped from belt to crotch. The waistband and belt were keeping the two legs together. We laughingly hurried to the first house in sight. A kind lady and her teenaged daughter were the only people at home. Alex explained my predicament and we were quickly invited to come in. They provided me with a room where I removed my trousers and Alex took them downstairs. I could hear the sewing machine in operation and in no time my mended trousers were returned to me. This occurred in Heatherton and after we had coffee and sandwiches we continued our crusade.

I spent some time in White Bay South, and soon the campaign period came to an end. I returned home to Gander for polling day.As was the case in 1971, Gander was the first district to be announced by the media. The final count was: Collins 4,674; Baker 2,272; Boone 177. A total of 77% of the Gander District eligible voters marked their "X." The provincial result was just as overwhelming. The Conservatives under Frank Moores captured 33 of the 42 seats for a clear and undisputed mandate.Listed among the casualties were Tom Burgess and Hugh Shea. Such was the beginning of the first Progressive Conservative Government since Confederation in 1949.

~ Chapter Forty-five ~

End Of The Smallwood Era

The Progressive Conservative victory of 1972 marked the end of the Smallwood era in Newfoundland politics. We held 33 of the 42 seats and 60 % of the popular vote.

The Liberals under their new leader, Ed Roberts, held the remaining 8 seats.

The anti- Smallwood vote of 1971 became a pro- Progressive Conservative vote in 1972. Newfoundlanders were anxious for political change and even traditional outport Liberal strongholds supported us. During its 3-1/2 years in office, the Moores administration compiled a steady but unspectacular record. In contrast to the flamboyant years of Smallwood, Moores was quiet and business like. His administration was seen as a working government, cleaning up the Liberal mess which we had inherited. Some of our major achievements were: the purchase of majority shares in the Churchill Falls power project from the Brinco Corporation; strong consumer protection legislation; strong forest management legislation and improvements in the pulpwood industry; improvements in educational facilities (in 1975, $21.4 million was spent by government on new school construction, $17.2 million for Memorial University`s new teaching and General Hospital, and $500,000 towards construction of a new polytechnical school).

In spite of these achievements, the unemployment roll was still high, inflation was rising and revenues failed to keep up with expenditures. Moores was convinced that government popularity would wane as the months rolled by. The Liberals under Roberts were in disarray and there was every indication Smallwood would form a reform Liberal party and no doubt split the Liberal vote.

Moores was a canny politician and engaged a professional polling organization to measure the political scene for him. In time he decided to go to the people and called an election for September 16,1975. A Redistribution Act had been passed since the 1972 election, and the province was now divided into 51 districts. The old Gander District became two, Botwood, Northern Arm, Peterview and Bishop`s Falls, along with Leading Tickles and Fortune Harbour became the District of Exploits. Gander, Glenwood, Appleton, and Benton comprised the new District of Gander.

I elected to run in the District of Gander and my opponents were Averill Baker, Liberal, and Lowell Paulson, NDP. I won the seat with a total of 2,462 votes and there were 1,852 for Baker and 250 for Paulson.

The day after Smallwood resigned in January 1971, Premier Frank Moores invited me to his Cabinet as Minister of Municipal Affairs and Housing. I remained in that portfolio until after the 1972 election. In the years 1972 and 1973 the government spent more money on water and sewer projects than ever before in our history. A new cost-sharing program for municipal road construction was also implemented. The Newfoundland and Labrador Housing Corporation was strengthened and expanded. Several new housing projects in St. John`s, Burin, Marystown, Gander and Corner Brook were brought to construction.

The development of municipal government in Newfoundland and Labrador was not a priority of the Smallwood government. His obsession with industrial development, " the development or perish philosophy" took precedence over everything. Coupled with his disastrous resettlement program, which left the future of many settlements in limbo, much work needed to be undertaken. Many incorporated communities were on the verge of bankruptcy and dozens of other communities were lined up to become incorporated, thinking it was the sure way to obtain water and sewer services. During my term as Minister more water and sewer systems were completed and started than ever before. More Local Improvement Districts (an outdated form of local government) were converted to elected councils. Despite all of these improvements, the development of municipal government in Newfoundland still lagged behind other jurisdictions in Canada. It soon became evident that some conceptual changes were needed. With this in mind, I suggested to my colleagues the establishment of a Royal Commission. The Lieutenant Governor in Council agreed and Professor Hugh Whalen was appointed Chairman of the Royal Commission on Municipal Government in Newfoundland and Labrador. The two members of the Commission were Mr. Clarence Powell, a former Deputy Minister of the Department, and Mr. Hubert Harnett, a chartered accountant and former City Councillor in Corner Brook. The Royal Commission's Terms of Reference were sufficiently broad to permit it to study, evaluate and report on all aspects of municipal government. While I had moved to another department by the time the report was received, it became the blueprint for development of municipal government in the province.

Perhaps the most important piece of legislation which I introduced was the May 1, 1973, Act Further to Amend the City of St. John's Act. It might come as a surprise to readers to realize that only property owners in St. John's were permitted to vote in city elections. Universal suffrage applied in all provincial and federal elections. The principal also applied to municipal elections in all other towns in the province. In St. John's, owners of several properties held blocks of votes, which meant that they could strongly influence the election of the mayor and councillors. The first Progressive Conservative government resolved to correct that injustice. It was a proud day for me when I introduced the bill, an Act to Amend the City of St. John's Act on May 1, 1973, which gave all citizens 19 and over the right to vote for the mayor and councillors. For the first time in history, St. John's women and others were enfranchised to vote in city municipal elections.

When I was appointed Minister of Municipal Affairs & Housing, the Town of Gander was the envy of every municipality in the province. Having served on that town council for three terms, it was predicted that I would give Gander special status. Naturally, I had to be seen to be treating all municipalities alike but one would have to be naive to think that Gander District would be shortchanged, and I saw to it that didn't happen. I developed a good working relationship with all councils in the province. Councils in my own district were treated well and appreciated what I was doing. Northern Arm, Peterview, Botwood, Glenwood and Appleton were well served. The same could not be said for Gander. Not only did Gander council refuse to cooperate with me and the officials of my department, they chose the route of open confrontation at every opportunity. The sad reality of all this was that the people of Gander suffered. There were two reasons for the lack of cooperation on the council's part. First, the majority of the councillors and the town manager, Mr. Baker, were confirmed Liberals; secondly, they wanted me to get no credit for anything done in Gander. Doug Sheppard, a relative and a member of council, had already run against me and lost. I had defeated Mayor Robertson. Town manager, Eli Baker, was next and he was also badly beaten. The old adage, if you can't beat them, join them, became if you can't beat them, embarrass them.

The first opportunity to do that arose in 1972. There was a by election in Gander and Sgt. Bernard O'Leary, a member of the Canadian Forces stationed at Gander, contested the election and won a seat on council. I was forced into dismissing the council but minutes before that was to happen they all resigned. An interim council was appointed to administer the affairs of the town, and a new election was called as soon as possible. Most of the old councillors were defeated.

In 1972, Hotel Gander was the site for the Progressive Association of Newfoundland's annual meeting. It was one of the largest functions ever to take place in Gander. Unfortunately, it was marred by a serious outbreak of fire at the hotel. While there was no loss of life, rescue efforts were hampered by virtue of the fact that the fire department did not have an aerial ladder. Premier Moores and my colleagues in cabinet instructed me to do what I could to have an aerial ladder provided. Gander Council was requested to make application for assistance under the Fire Fighting Program. I rushed approval of the application and funds were arranged. While applications from other municipalities were ahead of Gander, the hotel fire was reason enough to give Gander priority. The Volunteer Firemen's Association of Newfoundland and Labrador was holding their annual meeting in Gander and I was invited as guest speaker. I chose that time to announce the acquisition of the fire truck and ladder. In fact, it was brought to Gander and demonstrated, and I informed Gander Council I would be making the announcement. To deny me any credit, the council decided they would not share in the cost and would not accept the fire equipment. This is another indication to what level they would stoop to embarrass me. Of course once again the people of Gander lost and the fire equipment went to Harbour Grace. Despite the total lack of cooperation from council, I served Gander well and saw to it, if necessary, that we circumvented the town council. Two new schools, the vocational school, hospital improvements, the Arts and Culture Center, stadium assistance, assistance to EPA, housing and street development, and relocation of government agencies are all monuments attesting to that.

Chapter Forty-six

Cabinet Shuffle

In 1973, Premier Moores reshuffled his cabinet. Roy Cheeseman, MHA for Fortune-Hermitage, had been Minister of Fisheries. He resigned his portfolio and his seat and I was appointed to succeed him. I don`t suppose there was ever a member of the House of Assembly who wouldn't jump at the chance to be Minister of Fisheries and I was no exception. The fishery was, and is, of such paramount importance, economically and socially, that it affects the lives of all of us.

Fisheries is a shared jurisdictional area. Federal fisheries has the prime responsibility for the management of the resource and harvesting . The provincial area of responsibility is in the processing and marketing of the products. Jack Davis, a Liberal Member of Parliament from British Columbia, was federal fisheries minister at the time. Jack and I got along extremely well. It was during my term as fisheries ministers that the initial groundwork was laid for the extension of Canada`s jurisdiction to the 200 mile continental shelf.

To say the Liberal government of Mr. Smallwood attached little importance to the Newfoundland and Labrador fishery would be untrue. To say they relied to a great extent on federal initiatives is true. As a consequence, we had a very weak and entirely inadequate provincial Department of Fisheries. The people who made up the department staff were dedicated. but they lacked numbers and, above all, lacked direction and purpose. One of my first tasks was to build a strong department. Those hired included Rupert Prince, Joe Burden and Gordon Slade. We soon had the best provincial Department of Fisheries in Canada, and the federal government supported us.

Don Jamieson, Newfoundland's representative in Ottawa, was most helpful. Sometimes we could get along with Don better than we could with our own party people. Jointly with the Feds, we embarked upon a Marine Service Program. The centers at Old Perlican, Wesleyville, Twillingate, LaScie, Port Saunders, Harbour Grace and others, are part of that program. Numerous community stages, haulouts and slipways were also constructed. All of these services were essential and appreciated by fishermen. The Fisheries Loan Board was enlarged and strengthened and the Fishing Industry Advisory Board was established. Several new processing plants were established and improved fishing techniques introduced. One of the more forward looking accomplishments was the provision of a floating barge which was placed at Smokey on the Labrador Coast. This barge brought salt, gear, and food to Labrador fishermen in that area. I am very proud indeed of my accomplishments as Minister of Fisheries.

Now to some of the more unpleasant experiences during my term as Minister of Fisheries. Since time immemorial the Newfoundland fishery has been subjected to severe cyclical upturns and downturns. Catches have varied from a glut in one year to a paucity in the next year. Fluctuations in prices were just as severe. Never could high prices and high landings be matched up. Fishermen, however, remained optimistic, always looking forward to next year being successful.

Not only were our fishermen faced with severe price and landing fluctuations, they had to contend with a sometimes savage environment. Storms and ice, dirty water and dogfish were a few of the problems. Wind and sea storms and ice can inflict terrible damage to fixed gear and shore facilities and boats. Such was the case in 1974. The Northern ice was moving in and out of the bays all spring. In a desperate effort to land fish, fishermen took chances. Their reward was damaged boats, battered shore facilities, and lost and damaged traps and nets. Conditions were so bad that on July 9 it was possible to walk from Cape St. Francis to Baccalieu and on north to Cape Bauld on ice. Similar conditions existed along the coast of Labrador.

In the middle of July, Premier Moores and I used a helicopter to visit communities in Conception, Trinity and Bonavista bays. The next day, we went to Musgrave Harbour, Wesleyville, Fogo, Twillingate and Triton. All of these areas were still blocked with ice, a devastating condition.

Pressures were mounting for a gear replacement program. It was clear if our fishermen were to ever fish again, a gear replacement program would have to be implemented quickly.

Cabinet approved an amount of $2 million as an emergency fund. A committee was established to investigate and report on losses. The Premier and I went to Ottawa. We met with Mr. Jamieson and Prime Minister Trudeau, and the federal government agreed upon a cost-shared program of assistance. The program was quickly put in place but, unfortunately, it was abused by some people. Investigation revealed abuses of such serious proportion as to demand prosecution. Some businessmen were charged and brought to court and found guilty of abusing the program. Fines and jail sentences were levied. Some of the media, particularly CBC, directed much criticism at government, and at me particularly, for implementing a program which couldn't be controlled. The criticism directed at me was so intense that the printed media came to my defense.

Our system assumed that people were honest and affidavits were required. In some cases, the honor system failed. In retrospect, I have no apologies, my conscience is clear. If faced with a similar emergency in the future, naturally I would require some changes in control. I can take great solace from the fact that, without our program at that time, hundreds of fishermen would have had to retire from the fishery.

In the fall of 1974, the Premier decided to make a somewhat major cabinet shuffle. When the dust had settled I was Minister of Forestry & Agriculture. In addition I was also responsible for Crown Lands. The new forestry management legislation had just been proclaimed. Forest management units were established across the province. The portfolio was appropriate for a member from central Newfoundland, and I was looking forward to my term in that department.

The summer of 1975 was a terrible dry summer and we were plagued with many severe forest fires, both on the island and in Labrador. During that year, we were obliged to assist the struggling sawmill industry and a subsidy was paid to our potato farmers. The concept of cottage lots was introduced and favourably received, especially in St. John`s and Gander areas. A new potato seed farm was opened near Glenwood and Newfoundland Farm Products opened a new abattoir at Corner Brook.

After a couple of days of briefing and meeting staff people, I settled down to my new position. Forestry was the most important part of the portfolio, from an economic point of view. Ed Maynard, my predecessor, had just brought in the new forest management legislation. I immediately began to follow through with the establishment of regional offices and the many managerial units which were needed. Much of our work was related to the two big paper companies at Grand Falls and Corner Brook , the Labrador Linerboard Mill at Stephenville, and logging operations in Labrador. As well, there were the many small sawmill operators who needed saw logs, and the individual contractors who supplied wood to the paper mills. While the paper companies had their own forest lands, we had to try and find wood for the others from Crown Land. Our Resource Roads Program opened up many areas of the province for this purpose.

The farmers of Newfoundland always thought the department paid more attention to forestry and not enough to agriculture. This was not true because great efforts were expanded in agriculture, although we never received the credit due.

In the summer of 1975 we had some major forest fires in Labrador. The worst was at Charlottetown where people were evacuated on two occasions before the fires were brought under control. If forest fires were a problem in 1975, conditions in 1976 were catastrophic. It was a very dry summer and it seemed as if the whole island and Labrador were on fire. The areas of greatest concern were Rattling Brook, Northwest Gander and Northern Arm, Botwood. The paper companies and the government spared no effort in fighting all the fires, and eventually they were brought under control, but not before there were major timber losses.

~ Chapter Forty-seven ~

The Government Ram

In days gone by most Newfoundlanders kept a few sheep, just as we did on Indian Islands, and some people kept a lot of sheep. Over the years, inbreeding resulted in smaller animals. The result, less wool and less meat. There was a need for some new blood. Suggestions were made to the government and to their credit they introduced the following program.

Top quality rams were imported from prime Scottish stock to breed the Newfoundland ewes. People desiring the services of a ram were advised to get in touch with the Agricultural Division of the Dept. of Natural Resources. Since there was a limited number of rams available, the earlier the applications were made the better the chances to get a ram.

A fellow in a small community on the northwest coast made application in the spring of the year. He heard nothing in reply so he wrote the division head again. Still he received no reply. He decided to write the minister, which he did and waited for a reply. Sure enough in a matter of days he received a reply. The minister apologized for the fact that the previous letters went unanswered. He then proceeded to tell the gentleman why his request could not be acceded to.

The government had only six rams and these had to be distributed in October to the largest communities. His community lacked population numbers to qualify under the program. He quickly fired off a telegram to the minister which read as follows:

"Received your letter today concerning unavailability of ram due insufficient people in this community. I want you to know that we wanted the ram for the sheep not the people. Can you kindly reconsider?"

I saw this correspondence when I was Minister of Agriculture in 1975-76, and I could never establish if the man ever did get the ram.

~ Chapter Forty-eight ~

Department of Health

The greatest challenge of my political life took place in 1976, when the Premier asked me to become Minister of Health. I was visiting my home town of Gander when the call came. I expressed some reservations and made reference to the fact that it was a department of medical professionals. He said being a professional politician, I should have no problems.

I returned to St. John`s and was sworn in the next day at Government House. The following day I moved to the department. Tom Sellars, one of the senior public servants in government, was the Deputy Minister of Health. He introduced me to the departmental staff and began the briefing. During my time as Minister of Health, the first Detoxification Center in the province was opened in St. John`s as was the Health Science Centre. The new hospital at Twillingate and the new and enlarged Western Memorial Hospital were also opened. The old Western Memorial Hospital in Corner Brook was converted to a high level service unit for the care of geriatric patients, the first such facility in the province. Work was also started on converting the old General Hospital in St. John`s into the Leonard A Miller Centre. The USAF hospital at Goose Bay was turned over to the province, and then to the International Grenfell Association. The new Waterford Hospital was opened in St. John`s.

In addition to being Minister of Health in 1976- 1978 I was also Minister of Social Services, and Minister of Rehabilitation and Recreation. At this time I was also chairman of the social policy committee of cabinet and a member of the planning & priorities committee of cabinet.

I soon became painfully aware of the need to consolidate some essential services of these three departments under one department. The Department of Health was responsible for the general delivery of health care in the province. However, the federal funds for mental health and child rehabilitation were channeled through the Social Services Department. Homes for the care of the elderly were operated by the Department of Rehabilitation, even though a fairly high level of health care was provided. It seemed to me that the health care dollar would give more benefits if all three of these departments were to become one. Had Premier Moores not resigned, I believe we would have brought this about. But he did resign, a new premier came on, and I was moved from health. To Premier Brian Peckford`s credit, he did consolidate Social Services and Rehabilitation. It is a pity he did not go all the way and create the Ministry of Health and Social Services, or at least Health and Institutions, leaving Social Services to its own department.

During the years of the Moores administration, Frank and I developed a very close working relationship fostered on a mutual respect for each other. Some of Premier Moores detractors, and he had many, would have us believe that he was nothing more than a playboy and was lacking in a work ethic. My response to is that it was through his hard work and determination that we formed the first Progressive Conservative government since Confederation with Canada. It was a sad day for me when Moores announced his resignation on January 19,1979. At the same time he announced a leadership convention for March 17. My good friend Brian Peckford won the nomination and was sworn in as Premier on March 26 the same year. Brian immediately offered me the environment portfolio and I accepted but I had a gut feeling my days in government were rapidly coming to an end. Brian called an election for June 18 and over some very strong objections from my friends and supporters I decided I would not be a candidate. I assisted Brian in finding a candidate to replace me and Hazel Newhook was elected in Gander District.

After the election Joan and I took some time away from it all and we decided that perhaps I should return to Canadian National. I was still on leave of absence from the company. I met with Jack Gosse, district manager, and he offered me a new public relations position with my office in St. John's, even though company headquarters was now located in Gander. I carefully considered the offer but declined and subsequently submitted my resignation to Canadian National. Premier Peckford then indicated to me that he would like me to take on the position of Chief Protocol Officer for the Province. I agreed to take him up on the offer and assumed the position. Some of the more interesting people I entertained included Paul Robinson, the United States ambassador to Canada, Marc Garneau, our first astronaut, and the crew of the U.S. spacecraft, Columbia.

In 1985, I accepted an invitation from Prime Minister Brian Mulrooney to serve as the chairman of the Canadian Fisheries Prices Support Board, a position I held to 1990 when I resigned. By then, I had completed 50 years in the workforce and considered a change would be good for me.

Today, with our 10 children all left the nest, Joan and I can be found at 34 Dunfield Street in St. John's.

~ Chapter Forty-nine ~

An Old Friend Called

It was one of those warm days in the east end of St. John's in July 1988. Joan and I had spent most of the day in the back garden mowing the grass and attending our flowers. The pleasant weather extended into the evening and we fired up the barbecue and enjoyed our evening meal outside in the fresh air. Around 10 p.m. we retired to the living room, and I was endeavouring to catch up on local world events as reported by the Telegram when the telephone rang. The voice on the other end inquired if I was Harold Collins and when I answered yes, he asked me if I was the Harold Collins from Indian Islands, and when I again answered in the affirmative he said, " Are you the man who was in politics?" and I said yes and asked who I was speaking with. He said, "I'm John Bishop," and I said, "The John Bishop who once taught school on Indian Islands?" and he answered that yes it was. I was rather dumbfounded and asked him where he was calling from and he told me he was calling from his sister's house in the city. I asked him for the address and found out he was at the corner of Springdale Street and LeMarchant Road. He said he was leaving on the early morning flight and would appreciate seeing me before he left. I was so excited I jumped in the car and took off for that address and didn't even tell Joan where I was going or whom I was to meet. When I arrived at John's sister's address she and her husband and John were sitting on the front steps. John and I shook hands and I met his sister and husband for the first time. John picked up his luggage, they exchanged goodbyes and John and I left for my house.

Joan had heard me speak about John Bishop several times over the years but she had never laid eyes on him before, and she was fascinated by our discussions during the wee hours of the morning. You see, John was my last school teacher in the school year of 1938-39 and I had never heard from him since that year. I wanted to know what he was doing in St. John`s and where he was going so early in the morning. He told me he was now retired and living in Boston, Mass. and then followed what was a very exciting story. He said he owned a yacht and did a fair amount of sailing. He would like to do more but his wife was a landlubber and very seldom accompanied him. His sailing mate was their only child, a daughter who spent a lot of time with him on the boat up until she got married. He then decided he would get rid of the boat and spend more time on land with his wife. He solemnly promised her he would do that but before letting the boat go he wanted to sail to Newfoundland. It was agreed his daughter and husband would accompany him on the trip and after much planning they left Glouster, just outside Boston, in the early days of July. They sailed down the Atlantic coast to Halifax. They thought they would spend a few days in that port and then sail for the island. His son- in- law contacted his office and was surprised to find that he was required to return to Boston as soon as possible. They discussed the problem and it was decided that his daughter and husband would abandon the journey and return home. John was determined to continue and over the objections of his family he did just that. The next morning he slipped the moorings and left Halifax. He sailed across the Cabot Strait up the west coast and through the straits of Belle Isle. I knew he was headed for the east coast and I interrupted his story by asking why he took that route. He replied, "I always wanted to see the west coast and since Indian Islands were on the north east coast I thought that was a sound decision." I then asked, "Why did you go to Indian Islands? " He replied, "I always regarded Indian Islands as my home." He referred to the fact he was only sixteen years old when he came there and boarded with us. He said, " Your parents and all the family accepted me as one of your own and I never forgot that." I thought that was more than kind of him but I could appreciate where he was coming from. Anyway, he continued his excursion down the east coast and just as darkness was setting one evening he arrived at Indian Islands. After he had anchored in the tickle he had some doubts whether he was in the right place, but according to his charts he was in fact at Indian Islands. He retired after a long day's sailing and when he arose in the morning it was well past daylight and he was shocked to find he was indeed in the right place but there were no houses or any other sign of life and he wondered what had happened. He was unaware the people had resettled years ago. When he finished breakfast he hauled anchor and sailed over to Seldom on Fogo Island. He tied his boat to the old Fisherman's Trading Company wharf and inquired of the first person he encountered what had happened to the people who lived on Indian Islands. He was informed that the people resettled in the mid-fifties. He realized my parents would have departed this world and when he inquired about me he was told I was living in St. John`s and they told him of my political career and thus the telephone call. The few hours we had together passed all too quickly. He told me that following his year at Indian Islands he accepted a position at Joe Batt`s Arm on Fogo Island but stayed there for the first term only. He took the second term to ponder his future. His father was also a teacher and during that summer it was agreed John should go to University. He applied for and was accepted at McGill in Montreal. After his first term at McGill, the Dean called him to his office and told him he was wasting his time there. John was a bit shaken but the Dean convinced him he should set his sights on Harvard and in January he transferred to Harvard Business School, regarded as the top business school in the U.S. To make a long story short, John had much success there and subsequently became the Dean of that prestigious business university. On the way to the airport he told me he was leaving his boat at the Long Pond boat club in Conception Bay and planned to return later in the year and sail it back to Boston. We were out of town when he returned but I assume he sold the boat and is now retired and living in Boston.

End

THE PEOPLE OF EASTERN INDIAN ISLAND (that I recall)

1. Samuel and Leah Kinden

2. Nathaniel and Effie Kinden
   Children Marie, Harold, Eric, Ivy, Howard, Maryln and Judy

3. Leslie and Florila Kinden.
   Children Vera and Helen.

4. Baxter and Effie Boone.
   Children Blanche, George, Harvey and Frank

5. Eliza Kinden and Charlie (deceased)
   Children Roland and Charles.

6. Archibald and Matilda Roberts.
   Children Lucy, Laura, Eloise, Ruby and Nathaniel.

7. Wilson and Mary Sheppard.
   Children Glen, David and Elizabeth.

8. Stanley Kinden and Mary (deceased)
   Children Stella, Gordon, Ethel and Jessie.

9. Ernest and Emily Kinden.
   Children Ralph, Frank, Nary, Harold and Mark.

10. Pierce and Eliza Sheppard.
    Children William, Frank, Eva, Jessie, Cyril and Douglas.

11. Malachi and Emily Sheppard.
    Children Louie, Francis, Millicent and Phyllis.

12. Leonard and Janie Sheppard.
    Children Emily, Clarence and Thosms.

13. Simeon and Dorcas Sheppard.
    Children Litta, Alva, Otto, Eldon and Watson.

14. Allan and Annie Sheppard
    Children Doris, Herbert, Myrtle, Alice and Elmo.

15. Stephen and Helen Sheppard.
    Children Molley, Elsie, Bessie, Edgar and Malcolm.

16. George and Gertie Hynes.
    Children Raymond, Reginald , Richard, Aunt Maria George`s mother and Harvey Downer his nephew and wife Bessie.

17. Lorenzo and Bessie Collins.
    Children Lydia, Meta and Harold (myself).

18. Harvey and Vera Frampton.
    Children Yvonne, Allan, Earl, Marjorie and Florence.

19. Kenneth and Ivy Frampton.
    Children Marlyn and Beverly.

20. Walter and Jane Penney.
    Children Woodrow Guy (adopted)

21. Mark and Emily Vincent.
    Children Netta, Ivy, Lemuel, Hilda, Douglas and Frank Saunders (adopted).

22. Garland and Alfreda Penney.
    Children Edward, Lemuel, Augustus, Marjhorie, Roland and Wallie.

23. Charlie Will Penney.

24. Arthur and Effie Penney.

25. Albert and Grace Penney.
    Children Roland, Charles, Arthur, Kenneth, Clarence, Jane, Mildred and Elizabeth.

26. Edward and Ethel Penney.
    Children Jessie, Donald and Cyril, Father Mark and Brother Andrew.

27. George and Florrie Collins.
    Children Richard, Gwendolyn, Mary, Ida, George, Charles, Step-son Maxwell Rowe and Step-daughter Verlie Rowe.

28. Edith Collins and Moses(deceased).
    Children Sturdee and Bessie.

29. Walter and Eliza Collins.
    Children Kenneth and Jethro.

30. Maxwell and Nellis Collins.
    Children Rella..

31. James, Alfreda and Naomi Collins.

32. Solomon and Athea Collins.

33. Richard and Maria Collins.
    Children Lemuel, Stella and Effie.

34. Lemuel and Florence Collins.
    Children Horace, Stella and Olive.

35. Elijah and Dinah Collins.
    Children William.

36. John and Eva Collins.
    Children Albert, Jethro and Donald.

37. Albert and Leah Collins.
    Children Gordon, Fannie, Gilbert, Marion, Curtis, Reginald and Dinah.

38. Robert and Sarah Bixby.

39. John and Mabel Bixby.
    Children Marina.

40. Albert and Laura Cull.

41. John and Agnes Cull.

42. Ray and Dorothy Cull.

43. Jethro and Nora Cull.

44. William and Ella Cull.
    Children James and Clive.

45. Doug and Bessie Cull.

46. Eleazer and Lucy Coish.
    Children Donald, Boyd, Wilhilmena, Beth, Hazel, Olive and Margret.

Always A Straight Shooter

47. Harold and Stella Sheppard.

48. Art and Annie Sheppard.

49. Andrew and May Coish.
    Children Lloyd, Alex, Geraldine, Bessie, Maisie, Wilbert and Alvin.

50. Baxter and Verlie Coish.
    Children Max and Florence.

51. Alex and Selena Coish.

52. Henry and Jessie Ella Sheppard.
    Children Glenda, Lorne and Lester.

53. Arthur and Florence Frampton.
    Parents John and Jane.
    Children Bartram and Clifford

54. Jimmy John and Emma Perry.
    Children Mildred, Leander, Winston and Earl.

55. Kenneth and Sylvia Sheppard.
    Children Myrtle, Mary, Rose and Piney.

56. John and Violet Hoddinott.

57. Mark and Rachel Sheppard.
    Children Walter, Henry, Baxter, Art, Nathan, Harold, Roland, Len Don, Louise and Jessie.

58. Charles and Eliza Sheppard.

59. Walter and Harriott Sheppard.

THE PEOPLE OF PERRY'S ISLAND (Western Indian Islands) that Granville Hoddinott can personally recall from the late 1930's and early 40's

1. Mary Ann Hoddinott and Samuel (deceased)
   Children Walter and Lewis.

2. Bill-Jim and Martha Hoddinott.
   Children Ned, Sam, Jim.

3. Cecil and Myrtle Hoddinott.
   Children Lorraine and Allen, Brother George, Mother Susie.

4. William and Emma Hoddinott
   Children Burle, Roland Randolph, Betty and Ken.

5. Lemuel and Ida Hoddinott.
   Children Don, Wilf, Alice, Dot, Granville and Ivy.

6. Gordon and Evelyn Hoddinott.
   Children Wilf and Jean.

7. Roland and Betsy Hoddinott
   Children Pearl and Levi.

8. Elizabeth (Lizzy) Hoddinott.
   Children Lud and Sherman.

9. John and Winnie Gale.
   Children George, Greek, Mose, Irene, Holly and Maud.

10. Joe and Liddy Gale.
    Children Florence, Hatty and Audrey.

11. Tom and Dorcas Carnell.
    Children Ned, Eliga, Florence and Kelvie.

12. George and Betty Day.
    Children Harold, Ralph, Howard and Wavy.

Always A Straight Shooter

13. Richard and Scelena Carnell.

14. George and Ethel Rowe.

15. Will and Leany Perry.
    Children Jet, Guy, Billy Laura and Joyce.

16. George and Ethel Perry.
    Children Cyril, Cliff, Calvin, Ernest, Anne and Joan.

17. Nick and Jessie Perry and then his second wife Bessy Blundon.
    Children George, Ivy, Phyllis Blundon.

18. Al and Irene Collins.
    Children Armorel, Myrtle, Jean, Llewelyn, Eric and his wife Eloise.

These lists may not be complete and I apologize for any errors or omissions, with the passing of time memories do fade.

Harold's Parents

Lorenzo Collins

Bessie Sheppard

Always A Straight Shooter

Harvey's daughter, my niece Yvonne in front of our home, Indian Islands

St. Peter's Anglican Church, Indian Islands

Always A Straight Shooter

Uncle Joe Gillingham's horse with pot lids for snow shoes

Garden Rod fence like we had on Indian Islands

Family Photo: Back row L-R - Paul, Brian, David, Kevin, Betty, Debbie
Front row L-R - Derek, Craig, Harold, Joan, Sharon. Front Center - Tony

1966

Opening of Twillingate Hospital 1976
Dr. J.M Olds seated next to former Premier Smallwood, myself as M.C.

Harold and Frank Moores 1976

HAROLD COLLINS

Harold Collins was born in Indian Islands, located on the northeast coast of Newfoundland in Notre Dame Bay, in 1925 and lived there up until 1940 when he went to work as a wireless operator with the Department of Posts and Telegraphs. With Confederation in 1949 he became manager of Canadian National Telecommunications in Corner Brook. He moved to Gander in 1956, and was elected to the Gander town council in 1962. In 1967, he was elected to the House of Assembly as the Progressive Conservative representative for Gander district. Until his retirement from provincial politics in 1979 he served terms as Minister of Municipal Affairs and Housing, Fisheries, Forestry and Agriculture, Health, and Consumer Affairs and Environment.

Harold and his wife Joan (Peckford) are the parents of 10 children and currently live in St. John's.